I0894426

Concise guides to planning

Planning and Real Estate

Planning and Real Estate

Brendan Williams

LUND HUMPHRIES

First published in 2019 by Lund Humphries

Lund Humphries
Office 3, Book House
261A City Road
London EC1V 1JX
UK

www.lundhumphries.com

ISBN (hardback): 978-1-84822-355-4
ISBN (eBook PDF): 978-1-84822-359-2
ISBN (eBook ePub): 978-1-84822-360-8
ISBN (eBook Mobi): 978-1-84822-361-5

Concise Guides to Planning (Print): ISSN 2516–8177
Concise Guides to Planning (Online): ISSN 2516–8185

A Cataloguing-in-Publication record for this book is available from the British Library.

Copy edited by Pamela Bertram
Typeset by Jacqui Cornish
Set in Favorit
Printed in the United Kingdom

Image credits:
All figures and tables are from the author's own sources, with the exception of Figure 4, © Alamy Stock Photo, and Table 2 which is adapted from OECD (2017) *The Governance of Land Use in OECD Countries: Policy Analysis and Recommendations*. Paris: OECD Publishing.

Dedication
This book is dedicated to my wife Rhonda, my partner for life in all endeavours and whose love and support has always sustained me, and also to my boys Niall and Ciaran, the three lights of my life.

Contents

Foreword

One of the major changes in planning education in the past two decades is the growing importance attached to ensuring students get a good grounding in real estate development. Many planning practitioners looking at our current courses have told me how much they wished they could be brought up to date on real estate as it hadn't had such prominence when they were attending university.

It is for this reason in particular that I am so enthusiastic about this book, which provides a hugely valuable introduction to real estate by a highly respected academic who also brings considerable practice experience as a surveyor, Brendan Williams. It is highly readable, hugely informative and filled a real gap in my education. It manages to combine important contextual material with some detailed worked up examples of valuation techniques. It is quite unlike any book in the field in its lucidity, brevity and high standards of illustration. I like too that Brendan brings to the book his own interests and values around sustainability and social justice, without preaching or straying from the core purpose of the book.

I suspect there are many, many others in my boat, needing a book like this – both planners wanting to know more about how the world of real estate works so they can enter into negotiations better informed – and development professionals who want to know more about how the planning system works. I rather think students will like it too as a primer for their studies.

Enjoy this book – I did! - and keep an eye out for other books in this series to help round out your professional knowledge and bring you up to date with current academic debates.

Graham Haughton, Series Editor

Preface

This book helps planners to develop their understanding of the development process and developers to understand the way planners view their role in relation to development. Since the Great Financial Crisis (GFC), the role which real estate and development finance played in the banking and economic crisis has brought increased public policy focus to those activities.

The planning and the development of local areas, managing and protecting the environment and the operations of the real estate markets can be viewed as both complementary and competing processes. Development is historically led by local economic circumstances with commercial and corporate pressures. The development and supply of space is essential for all aspects of human activity and planning control processes, such as zoning, density and height controls, which underpin supply decisions, and are frequently the subject of negotiations, cooperation and conflicts.

A symbiotic relationship has emerged in many jurisdictions with political, property and planning interests combining in the delivery of necessary development. Negotiations between developers, community interests, investors and planners can be assisted by an understanding of the alternative views and perspectives on the development process. These relationships in the recent period have become more complex with the impacts of the globalisation of investment flows. This has resulted in a major reconfiguring of the relationship between local, regional and global development and policy processes. The trend towards a global integration of urban property markets is driven by the international financing of major projects which directly influences the scale and style of real estate development.

The following chapters explore such relationships and how development gains are made and shared in the planning process and whether this aligns with the aspirations of planning policies. Many jurisdictions have a planning approach based on a localised development control model as evolved in the UK and Ireland and rooted in the common law. This results in administrative and planning systems rooted in strong property and development rights, and it is this model and the resulting real estate market outcomes that are the primary focus of this book.

Acknowledgements

Planning and Real Estate has evolved from my teaching on Planning and Real Estate Development programmes at University College Dublin (UCD) over recent years and my previous urban development research, as well as earlier experience as a chartered surveyor along with my work on publications in related areas listed in the references. The chapters on real estate appraisal have drawn on examples and discussions in my chapters in *Partnerships in Urban Property Development* by N. Dubben and B. Williams, along with earlier material from *Development Properties* by J. Ratcliffe and B. Williams, while the discussions on the role of the public sector and planning interventions in property markets include materials developed from *Urban and Regional Economics* by B. Williams and A. Reynolds-Feighan.

My thanks to James Barry at UCD and Rochelle Roberts at Lund Humphries for assistance with graphs and images, while photographs used are from a UCD project on Urban Development in Dublin by Brendan Williams and Ian Boyle.

Thanks also to Val Rose, commissioning editor at Lund Humphries, and to Graham Haughton, series editor, for their constant support and advice throughout this project.

Chapter 1 Public Policy, Planning and the Property Market

Making places and spaces

The outcomes of planning and real estate development decisions are of fundamental importance to all the inhabitants of a city or a region, since the making of places and spaces impacts on everyday life and the future wellbeing of communities. Planners have a dual role in helping set out aspirations for an area and providing a regulatory framework that helps guide future development. Planning systems can attract support and criticism from multiple political and public policy perspectives – a healthy sign of a functioning democratic system. Planning policies can be viewed by supporters as an essential framework for the creation of the physical structures within which society operates, while others criticise them as an unnecessary constraint on the property development market, delaying and blocking supply processes. Alternatively, planning systems may be viewed as a necessary democratic control of the real estate development process or, by some detractors, as uncritically supporting real estate and business-led development coalitions operating at the expense of local communities.

The importance of land-use planning rests in its leading role in providing the physical framework within which we live and work. The use of planning policy decision-making within competitive property markets is examined in this chapter, along with the role of regulation or interventions aimed at achieving equity and/or efficiency. The chapter will explore the evolving role of the state in the context of property markets in a market economy. This discussion will include recognition of the growing importance of environmental policy frameworks for property development. Specific issues of importance include: availability of zoned and serviced lands, infrastructure requirements, access to services and utilities, industry capacity and constraints and general policy environment, taxation, and regulation. The discussion will include examples of public policy influences on property markets through regulation and state intervention.

In land-use planning approaches the focus is on achieving an efficient use of resources, including land resources. By providing a framework for future infrastructure to support future development, planning can also improve the efficiency in the use of the financial resources of both public sector and private investors. The scope of the planning and public policy system has historically addressed broader social problems and issues of economic development and equality in an integrated manner. Planning systems based on a land-use control approach, as have evolved in the UK and Ireland, place a heavy reliance on market processes to achieve desired development objectives. The exploration of the key features of such systems and the relationships that exist between planning, public policy, real estate and finance interests is a key task of this book.

Comparing this land-use control planning model with other approaches can reveal differences in scope of powers, resources and administrative structures, as outlined in Chapter 2. It also highlights that evidence of improved planning and development outcomes can be identified based on alternative approaches and resourcing models. At opposite ends of the spectrum might be the historically integrated approach to social housing as the policy approach adopted in Vienna, Austria, as against the housing of lower socio-economic groups or ethnic groups in problem estates in separated public provision and market provision in a neo-liberal context. Social inclusion from the inception of development policies along with market support may produce a more socially balanced outcome than either state centrally planned models such as the pre-1990s command economy approach, or a development-led free market approach, as in the recent property development booms and collapses in Spain and Ireland.

In general, this exploration views planning of land markets and governance structures in relation to real estate development as part of a wider public policy debate. The role of government can be both supportive and negative towards all sectors in communities and impact upon community and sustainability and economic development prospects in both the short and long term. Relevant issues include the role that planning, policy and development interest's play and the power or control each can exert over the development process. It is also critical to explore policy instruments related to planning, including development control at local and regional level, public financing and investments, property taxes and legal remedies to development problems.

Relevant real estate issues include economic issues, such as elasticity of supply, which is the capacity of the property industry to respond to increases in demand, market cycles, market controls, vacancies, abandonment of lands and sites, and issues of impacts on neighbouring occupiers. Costs, decision-making and the role of subsidies and growth controls all shape market-driven planning and development processes. From such theoretical considerations emerge major planning challenges such as achieving social equity in the city. The economics of residential location and the self-reinforcing nature of positive externalities or impacts of development in good neighbourhoods and of negative externalities, or blight, in depressed inner-city areas, make progress in achieving social equity difficult and complex. This demonstrates the importance of the spatial development dimensions of investment, disinvestment, and employment and education, and their critical importance to planning. The persistent focus on competing individual interests through an economic exchange market with values or rents distributing uses undervalues political, social, resource issues and other factors.

The descriptive nature of the land-use market models as presented in Figure 1 shows the *Bid Rent Process* by which the varieties of alternative land uses compete for the best locations for their land use. The various sector bids produce a

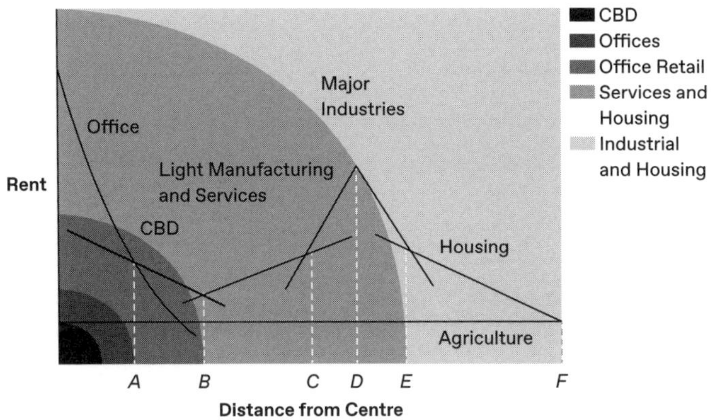

Figure 1
Urban land bid rent models

pattern of dominant land uses within urban areas. We can see – represented on the vertical axis – that commercial high-rent retail and offices become dominant in prime central business districts with the significant pull factors of central areas, while lower pricing patterns in standard housing and industrial sectors push these uses from such areas towards the suburbs on the horizontal axis.

A constant evolution in such market approaches, based on observed analyses of patterns of land uses and linkages within urban areas, have seen developments in key concepts including central place theories, agglomeration and concepts relating to land markets evolution.

The land market in an open market economy has the aim of optimising land use and profits and does not focus on the provision of equitable outcomes. Decades of planning and urban policy have sought to balance these market processes to achieve social and public improvements by influencing real estate outcomes. This policy approach to equity was traditionally focused on affordable housing and public amenities, and in modern times has included achieving lower energy consumption.

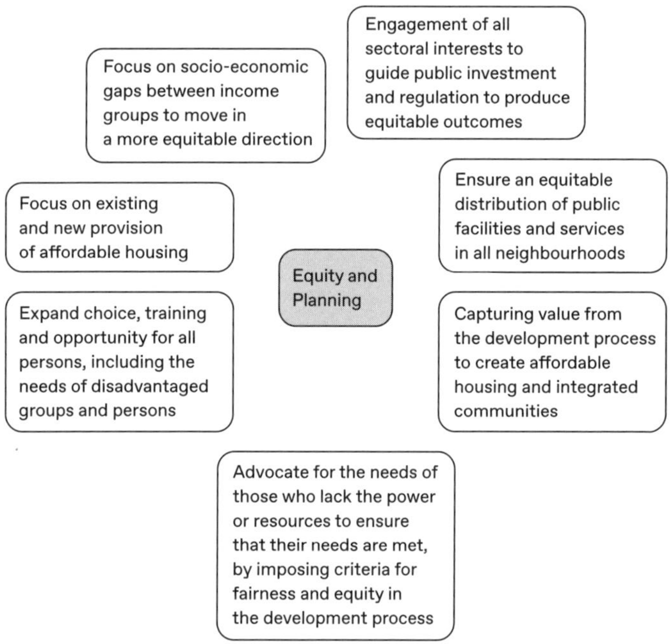

Figure 2
Equity and planning

In the modern period, the concept of equity and inequality has widened to include addressing socio-economic, ethnic opportunity and access issues, as illustrated in Figure 2.

Topics for critical evaluation include how we categorise planning and governance systems. Planning systems can be *pluralistic* and open to multiple local inputs, *regime-orientated* or controlled by *elites*. Communities and their elected representatives often claim that they are without power and resources to influence local development. For example, anti-austerity groups in European regions criticise urban policy-makers and processes as encouraging the financialisation of development processes in a neo-liberal economic context in ways that privilege elites and punish the undeserving, the poor and marginalised communities. This perspective sees the urban built environment as becoming a depository for investment capital, speculation and the commodification of housing and urban development, rather than providing essential housing, infrastructure and facilities.

A significant driver of modern planning policy internationally is the issue of environmental sustainability. Public awareness of environmental issues has led to a wide variety of UN, EU and international agreements on tackling major issues, including the long-term effects of climate change. Multiple programmes and planning policies attempt to put into effect such policies and become part of the mainstream of planning policy and practice. A problem for policy-makers in this area is that while the costs of such initiatives are often immediate and clearly identifiable, the savings in costs and times or revenues accruing are long term and less clear. Potential approaches to sustainability in planning are shown in Figure 3 and include the certification of new development which complies with prescribed standards, the introduction of energy coding for all buildings, and supports or

- Increased emphasis on sustainable growth-management strategies
- Increased density living areas and mixed residential and commercial uses in urban areas
- Growth management principles for smart city planning and design
- Reduced carbon development and smart growth
- Increasing walkability/cycling and built environments
- Increased use of Information and Communication Technologies (ICT) to create a sustainable built environment and smart cities research
- Clean and sustainable living environment
- Full life housing and living environments

Figure 3
Sustainability and planning

grants for upgrading existing buildings. The provision of grants for the retrofitting of older buildings with modern insulation materials and renewable energy appliances is increasingly promoted. This form of intervention is politically popular and can be argued to support local business and employment.

The consensus in the developed world on the approaches to regulate the use of limited resources through effective public policy and planning has lessened. Conventional approaches to the planning and development of urban areas have been viewed as deficient and the search for new ideas and approaches has led to the development of more market-led policies. It is therefore necessary to examine the conventional assumptions upon which urban policy has been based and why such approaches are perceived to have failed. The choice of policy and consideration of alternatives therefore necessitates investigation of the key themes or issues which underline the operations of property markets. Taking the example of inner-city dereliction: if it is a function of market malfunctions, government policies to loosen the constraints preventing such operations might suffice. If, however, the market is simply a reflection of deep-seated political, social or economic strains, broader-based policies tackling more difficult issues are required. The issue subsequently arises as to whether the various interest groups involved are willing to accept policies, including land-use planning, which would contribute to solving such problems.

Development problems, land use planning and the regulation of development

Historically, the evolution of planning policies and regulation of development in western nations was a reaction to the negative consequences of rapid urban expansion following the industrial revolution of the nineteenth century. The massive shift from agricultural to industrial employment created boom towns with large-scale manufacturing industry which developed without adequate guidance or control. The living conditions of the working classes and the squalor of the environment led to frequent outbreaks of disease – exposing the limits of market self-regulation – and calls for a greater role for the state. The lack of state regulation of housing development was identified as a cause of the severe health problems experienced by the new urban populations living in unsanitary conditions.

Public Health Acts formed the initial basis of planning approaches and were enacted in many European countries, including the UK and Ireland, to regulate and improve living conditions. Powers involved in such measures involved the enacting of bye-laws governing drainage, sewage, closure of unfit buildings and widths of streets. While in general the powers enacted contributed to higher standards of urban construction and improved layout in residential construction, more extensive planning of development did not occur until the twentieth century. Parallel with the development of public legislation, private philanthropists often developed highly individualistic concepts as to idealised forms of planned urban development. Notable amongst such developments in Britain were towns such as Saltaire, founded by Titus Salt (1851), Bourneville, founded by the Cadbury family (1895), and Port Sunlight, founded by W.H. Lever (1888). For example, the development of the mill town, New Lanark, in 1813 incorporated the provision of educational, health and social amenities. Such movements recognised the linkage between social and environmental problems in the creation and perpetuation of the problems prevalent in urban tenements or slums. Industrialists, amongst such philanthropists, also made the obvious link between improved living conditions for their workers and improved profits. Such movements recognised the linkage between social and environmental problems in the creation and perpetuation of the problems prevalent in poorly managed urban areas.

The role of the state in market regulation and direct intervention (such as slum housing removal) was intended as a positive and progressive process of regulation of development for the public benefit. This outlook contributed to the development of modern planning as based upon the idealism of the innovators of better models of urban development, such as the garden city movement, attempting to plan new developments to offer residents the benefits of both town and countryside. Town planning, in its modern meaning, involves analysing the overall physical development of the entire urban structure, and planning to accommodate its growth and development has developed from both an idealistic and a scientific base.

However, this historic analysis was challenged by many who viewed the state in a capitalist economy as being dependent upon, rather than a neutral regulator of, capital flows, consequently disciplined by the needs and requirements of capital. From such a critical perspective, this dependency creates an alternative role for state intervention as an agent to ensure social stability, compensate for market failure and regulate capital markets. Also notable from such early origins are the seeds of the later structuralist criticisms of the market capital economies which created such conditions (Harvey, 2011).[1]

The divergence of such views can be understood in the changing role of planning in the urban property markets and development management in many European and international jurisdictions. The optimism of early planning theorists can be readily identified in the work of some of its major exponents. Abercrombie, in the preparation of his civic plan for Dublin (1922) and the Plan for Greater London in 1944 (see Figure 4), planned for the development needs of the entire city region, including precise details of road developments, green space requirements, housing and all ancillary development needs.

The methodical basis of scientific survey, analysis and the mapped development plan became the standard model for development planning. A complex set of development standards was envisaged to ensure development control. Laid down in the development plan were standard features which remain operative in the modern system. These features include zoned and serviced lands, infrastructure requirements, and access to services, amenities, utilities and provision for modern industry capacity.

Central to the development plan approach as it emerged in the UK, the US and Ireland is the segregation of various parcels of land ascribed to broad classifications of land use, known as zoning. Zoning, combined with density controls, aims to

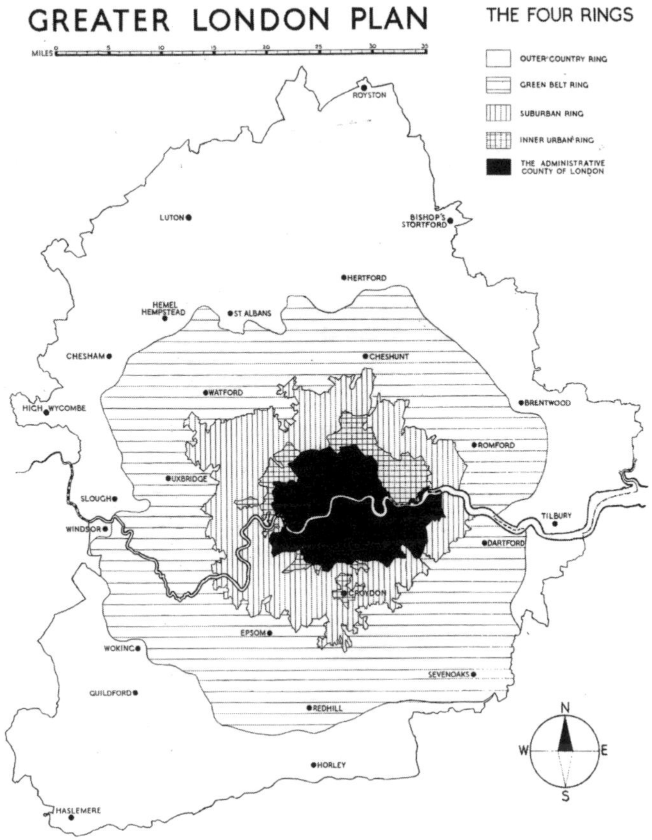

Figure 4
Greater London plan, showing rings of development

ensure maximisation of existing resources and segregation of incompatible uses, as outlined in Table 1. Densities are controlled, with ancillary guidelines covering the heights of buildings permitted, the amount of site coverage allowed and the relationship of the floor space area developed to plot size. Car parking standards can also be detailed, as are requirements for open space and amenities. Provision is made for future development of roads, services and infrastructure as well as development in obsolete areas. The role of the local and state authorities in the provision of social housing and public services will often be specified. All the above is represented on a series of land-use maps which forms the masterplan or blueprint for the area's development.

Zoning was originally based on the intention of segregating uses that were thought to be not compatible. With industrialisation in modern societies, the issue of public health concerns associated with air and water pollution, linked with factory emissions, emerged as a public policy priority. This led governments, through urban and city officials, to order functional separation of uses into zones or blocks where specific land uses were permitted, restricted or not permitted. Germany and Britain in the late-nineteenth century developed early zoning restrictions aimed at preventing polluting industries being allowed to operate in or near residential areas. Modern zoning can include wide categories of land use such as residential, mixed-use, combining residential and commercial, commercial offices, industrial, airports, retail, etc. Every category can be subdivided into several sub-categories, for example, industrial may be subdivided into heavy manufacturing, light assembly and warehouse uses. An example of a potential configuration of permitted land uses in zones or blocks in urban areas is presented in Table 1.

Table 1
Zoning

Commercial and Retail Uses	High-Density Residential	Low-Density Residential
Industrial – Warehouse Use	**Commercial Offices Central Business District**	Commercial and Retail Uses
Airport and Related Uses	Mixed-Use Residential and Commercial	Industrial – Light Manufacturing

Experience of this type of blueprint planning has led to criticism of such systems on the basis that rigid controls make such systems essentially negative in character in that they do not generate types of land use, although they may prevent improper or inappropriate use of land use and development. Extensive road widening, and improvements envisaged in such plans, frequently avoid the issue of streetscape replacement. The most serious criticism is that the approach can lead to a lowering of standards in that development complies with the minimum basic requirements, leading to monotonous and replicated forms of development, particularly of housing areas. Alternative models which allow greater flexibility in planning control depending on the quality of the development proposed, as in France and other jurisdictions, highlight the limitations of the fixed masterplan system.

The post-Second World War period saw the development in various continental European countries and the UK of the concept of comprehensive planning for urban property development. Across much of Europe, entire cities needed reconstruction following war damage, and concepts of planning for peace and redevelopment within a shared welfare state were readily politically and socially accepted. The role of policy interests was viewed as an arbiter of development in a way that was socially responsible. Scarce resources were to be allocated and directed towards their most beneficial use, drawing largely from the disciplines of architecture, design and civil engineering in a socialist reconstruction manner. Implementation of such plans was, however, in the hands of multiple public and private interests in market economy jurisdictions (Kynaston, 2007).[2]

The balancing of public and private interests has been a recurring feature of all attempts to ensure efficient spatial order of urban development in this way. The state or local authority attempts to predict the volume of future development and then co-ordinate and steer such development towards desired objectives. In providing roads, infrastructure and the necessary planning permission for appropriate land uses, the local planning authority controls the distribution of future development. As commercial and housing development is normally instigated by the private sector in many jurisdictions, the state has only a limited role in the final implementation of the development plan. Effectively, the state's role as an instigator may often terminate once infrastructure and services are provided.

The provision of infrastructure and the issue of development gain have never been fully resolved in the British or Irish legal systems. Examples from north-western Europe, particularly Scandinavian cities, of defined procedures for the acquisition of land for development purposes by state authorities can be cited as examples of potentially more efficient management of state infrastructure investment. The operations of the present system of zoning and re-zoning can be criticised as conferring considerable monopoly development values on selected landowners with increased costs, but without benefits for the community or landowners. Historically, attempts in the UK, from the Uthwatt Report in 1942 to the Community Land Act 1975, have failed to resolve this problem. Similarly, in Ireland, reports such as the Joint Committee on Building Land in 1985 have identified the conferring of unjustified development gain at the community's expense as a major fault of the development zoning system.

The issue of the creation of development value and its allocation has been a central controversy in the creation of all development plans. A full, free market approach is that all development value, no matter how it was created, belongs to the individual landowner and that any attempt to take it away from the owner would be unjust. Additionally, such an approach assumes that all infrastructure is created through forms of taxation which the landowner has already paid or contributed to.

The contrary argument is that, as the public, through its investment in infrastructure, creates all or at least much of the increase in development value, that development value should not be attributed to private individuals. Attempts to recoup development value would, however, raise the question of the state or local authorities' exposure to increased claims for development losses of other landowners caused by development decisions. Problems in administration, allied with political reluctance to tackle so problematical an issue, have ensured that limited modern policy measures, other than the taxation of capital gains in certain circumstances, have been realised in this area to date in many jurisdictions.

The extent of public confidence in planning and the ability of statutory authorities involved in tackling development problems has decreased significantly in recent decades. Their inability to implement past development plans, often coupled with the negative effects of previous development, undertaken especially in the housing area, has led to much criticism of planning failures. This criticism is often directed strongly at the local authorities who have statutory responsibility for planning and development within their areas.

The result of such criticism is that central government and interested parties internationally sought alternative forms and structures to deal with existing and emerging planning and urban development problems. Criticism of central government for planning failures is often less expressed, although often equally, if not more, justified. Reduction in budgets at national level, with decreased central subvention and support of services at local level, has been a frequent feature of central government policies from the 1980s through to the recent recessionary period from 2009 onward in many countries. In many jurisdictions the broad thrust of central government initiatives over many decades has been to reduce the financial resources and sources of funding for local authorities. This centralisation of power and resources reduced the ability of the local state authorities to deal effectively with development problems. Conflicts arose in areas where the central state government and local authority were controlled by different political parties, notably in the UK.

The combined results were that in the face of the mounting urban and property market problems of the twenty-first century, programmes, policies and initiatives had to be entirely reviewed. Often the existing agencies dealing with planning and development problems were found unsuitable and new approaches or specialist agencies were required. The reasons for such major review are often found in the complex and difficult pattern of social and economic problems which evolved in central or inner urban areas in recent decades.

In many ways, just as historical public health issues spurred the earlier development of planning in Europe and the developed world, similar challenges are now faced globally. In many parts of the globe, planning is needed for fast-growing cities and megacities in Asia and Africa and the rapid urban restructuring in North America or Eastern European cities. At the Quito Habitat Conference, members of the United Nations agreed to new guidelines to curb problems arising from rapid urban growth and established a set of common goals for urban development (UN, 2015).[3] Global challenges have been identified and agreed in the UN Sustainable Development Goals (SDGs).

The New Urban Agenda[4] is intended to assist planners and leaders in making cities more resilient. 'Urbanization is happening at an unprecedented pace and scale and 3.7 billion people now live in cities. We think in the forthcoming years, by 2050, this will rise to 7 billion,' Joan Clos, executive director of Habitat III stated. 'It is historic in the sense that never in human history have we seen such a transformation of human society,' he added, emphasising that the change represented a huge challenge to planners and leaders.[5] The UN has established that nearly one billion people live in urban slums in 100,000 cities in the world, often in precarious conditions. These people are in dire need of clean water, energy, food, sanitation and healthcare services. Learning from current and past planning policy and development experiences will hopefully assist in meeting these UN goals and indicators which reflect a key part of the future direction of planning policy internationally in the coming decade.

UN-Habitat has a stand-alone goal on cities as part of its sustainable goals agenda which is to 'Make cities and human settlements inclusive, safe, resilient and sustainable' as part of the 2030 Agenda for Sustainable Development.[6] It recognises that cities are a link connecting all other goals, with their density and economies of agglomeration linking economy, energy, environment, science, technology and social and economic outputs. These urban and regional interactions are viewed as essential in the formulation of integrated policies and planning to contribute to sustainable development.

Specific targets are expected to inform international planning and public policy debates in the coming decades, and indicated targets include:

- Indicator 11.1: 'By 2030, ensure access for all to adequate, safe and affordable housing and basic services and upgrade slums' with the indicator for measuring progress of 'Proportion of urban population living in slums, informal settlements, or inadequate housing'.
- 11.2: 'By 2030, provide access to safe, affordable, accessible and sustainable transport systems for all, improving road safety, notably by expanding public transport, with special attention to the needs of those in vulnerable situations and in terms of planning'.
- 11.3: By 2030, to 'enhance inclusive and sustainable urbanization and capacity for participatory, integrated and sustainable human settlement planning and management in all countries'.

The global importance of planning and real estate land use was also recognised in a major report by the OECD in 2017 which examined 'The Governance of Land Use in OECD Countries' with Policy Analysis and Recommendations.[7] This included a detailed survey on planning and land-use governance in 32 countries and found that land use is of increasing importance and a key policy area that can further economic, environmental and social goals. This is because land use has consequences for public health as it influences air quality and pollution; land and buildings account for the most important share of wealth in the OECD (86 per cent of the total capital stock) in 2017.

Land-use planning and existing urban areas – towards a reactive planning response

Planning systems are essential in managing the development of existing urban areas and built space as well as having a focus on controlling new development. Modern inner-city problems of stagnation and dereliction during growing economies had been a feature of US government priorities since the early 1960s, while recognition of such problems in Europe and action to alleviate them date mostly from the 1970s onwards. Across Europe, rehousing programmes and slum clearances, continuing since the post-war period, were by the 1960s leaving in their wake large areas of the inner-city vacant and derelict. The continuing priority of governments in Western Europe was housing, closely followed by infrastructure development, especially road building programmes.

The major problems identified were the movement of population to the suburbs, pollution and congestion making central areas unattractive for central city users, and the damaging effect on the urban fabric of the continued expansion of office space in central areas and infrastructural development to cope with increases in motorised traffic. A further common problem for development across the regions of Europe is that urban land suitable for public development projects is frequently prohibitively overpriced, partly due to compensation and legal provisions existing in various states.

Allied to the economic problems of urban areas are inner-area problems of congestion, poor urban management and site assembly difficulties where multiple historical legal rights exist to small plots of land and even within individual buildings. These, along with land remediation issues on former industrial sites, reinforce the effects produced by a lack of economic demand for built space and can lead to decline and dereliction. The timing of public interventions is also critical in city rejuvenation projects. The need for intervention to initiate and promote redevelopment can include land assembly assistance by compulsory purchase orders, grants and subsidies. However, as a development market matures, a singular focus on development promotion can be counterproductive as incentivised commercial development can be oversupplied and less profitable, but essential uses, such as affordable housing, are not prioritised.

The role of planning, which has evolved as a response of many governments internationally, has been a reactive one by which governments accept a role in dealing with the complex problems often raised by dysfunctional property markets. Planning was often introduced with the idealistic perspective of assisting economic and social progress with appropriate new development; however, the political will to reform the legislation and structures involved was lacking in many countries. Instead, the search for initiatives or programmes which will enable participants in the development process to surmount the inadequacies of existing planning and policy structures has emerged, especially relating to politically sensitive issues such as a lack of affordable housing.

Planning, public policy and the role of the state and local authorities are linked at every level to the property and urban development markets. The role of the state as provider of infrastructure and regulator of development involves achieving consensus between often powerful political and economic interests. Large imbalances exist between the various interest groups involved and their ability to exert power and influence over the political processes which govern urban development. The existence of such pressures is strongly evident in the nature and processes of planning regulation and development management which have evolved in many states.

Such pressures exist in most market economies and require strong and effective public policy structures to ensure that such influence does not favour sectional interest groups over the common good. The initiation and management of planning, housing and urban renewal programmes for central areas represents an area in which policy choices are many and difficult to evaluate. Careful monitoring and evaluation of such schemes is necessary at all stages to ensure that they are correctly focused to achieve their goals. The initiation and management of both housing and urban renewal schemes involves complex political decisions as to targeting, who benefits, and why. While opinions differ as to the relative merit of various approaches and packages, strong and effective local urban management structures greatly assist effective urban planning and development processes. Effective management of urban or regional transport, clear planning and infrastructure provision can create sustainable property markets but are often politically difficult to implement.

The public sector plays a significant part in all development activity in their role as planning authorities. In the UK and Ireland, the planning system is often mainly involved in issues of development control. This is often, in effect, a regulatory and restrictive role. As such, the role of the planning system as it has evolved, combined with the effect of local authority structures, can restrict the role of public intervention in the development process compared to other European jurisdictions. Participants in the development of the urban land market therefore often see planning as having a narrow, market-supportive role. Most private development interests are often willing to accept this control, in that it can improve the functional interaction between various land users. Such support is also based on intervention being necessary for development to take place in that the provision of physical infrastructure is necessary for further development, and regulating future development militates against haphazard and uneconomic patterns of activity.

The more restrictive operation of such public controls may in the longer term benefit development and investment interests in that it obviously affects the value of developments already made by creating entry barriers to the urban development market. For owners of existing developments, tight zoning and restrictive permissions for future new developments protect the long-term returns and capital values of existing property. Policies which tend to loosen restriction on market supply, while allowing investors to avail themselves of new opportunities in property investment, can obviously decrease property prices of existing property assets in the longer term. Policies which restrict development therefore can be viewed as supporting existing investments and property owners. Of course, if such restrictions go against a strong market trend – for example, strong demand for new office space in existing central locations – they can cause displacement of this sectoral demand to areas where permission is more readily available.

To restrict the role of planning to market-supportive measures in the longer term brings the planning system into a position of bargaining with development and investment interests. Dependent on development and investment interests for implementation of plans, the state and its planning functions are often seen as following market trends but being too weak to influence them. This dependency on capital and development interests for implementation significantly guides planning policy and gives dominant interests in the urban land markets a major role in planning urban areas. Criticism of such dependency sees the role of the state as dealing with the socially undesirable consequences of economic growth or lack of growth by changing its institutional or physical settings. This assigns a limited function to the state to fulfil those needs not addressed by market interests, such as housing for lower income groups. This role for the state can subsume major levels of finances and resources while private interests can concentrate to a greater extent on the benefit from growth and development, without sharing the wider costs and gains resulting from such new developments.

By its nature, planning control creates limitations on developments and conversely, monopoly value on sites zoned for high-value developments. It is these large windfall profits or latent value which attract development and investment interests. The distribution of this development gain obviously involves political choices and results in major financial rewards for some and losses for others. The argument that the community should have or share this gain is based upon that gain being dependent on public investment in infrastructure and basic services, and that the gain results from community growth and effort rather than private activity. The strong legal rights enjoyed by private property owners in many jurisdictions have as a compromise evolved systems of capital gains tax, which recoups part of such gains only through public taxation. The greatest pressures exerted on the planning system are frequently by land and property interests seeking to profit from development, and by residents who resist development as against their local interests. Also prevalent in such systems is speculation in property with development potential, where investors purchase or take options on property by identification of new development opportunity not already reflected by the market into the current price of that property.

Debates on planning and urban development trends and practice are often dominated by ex post analysis in which key factors are identified with hindsight bias to have been a cause of a trend, or events such as urban growth and transformations. These insights, often gained from policy debates and contexts in other jurisdictions, while useful, might then be used as a template to advise or predict what may be plausible future growth trends. If proved incorrect, this can be later supplemented by rationalisations or explanations when those template-based policies turn out to be wrong, resulting in stalled or partial regeneration of urban areas and the persistence of an affordable housing crisis.

Relationships between planners, developers and communities affected by planning policies are in a constant state of evolution and tension as planning decisions can result in sudden and permanent change in the built environment. These changes can greatly influence the lives of affected communities and the profitability of development interests, and are often subject to highly contested debates surrounding issues such as:

Market conditions and temporal issues, clearly in a reactive or market-led planning system the power dynamics vary greatly with strong or weak market conditions. Timing and phasing of development is a complex issue for both planners and developers. Combining short-term viability of individual development interests with long-term planning goals is difficult.

Spatially and geographically, where industry, market and planning policy aspirations for location of development often clash. Altering existing market sector preferences to achieve broader urban and regional goals requires long-term commitments from all partners in the planning and development process.

Ideological and cultural, where a conflict can exist as to the appropriate role of the state in regulation, direct development provision and the extent of market interventions. The contested nature of planning systems, and the changing political complexion of local authorities which govern such systems, gives rise to tensions at both local and national levels.

In conclusion, to increase their effectiveness, both planning and related urban and regional policies should be formulated based on clear conceptual thinking and strategic analysis. Programmes have in the past been developed on an ad hoc basis in response to sectoral demands and political imperatives. Examples of such trends include the major expansion of out-of-town shopping centres, fuelling auto-dependence and undermining core retail centres and existing high streets. In addition, recent moves towards higher rise residential developments in urban cores, without providing adequate ancillary services and new micro-parks and other public spaces, leads to concerns about inappropriate development suiting developers and investors rather than residential communities. The resultant pattern is that real estate development can be perceived as ad hoc or negative and damaging to the long-term planning and development of urban areas. The effects of urban policy on the production of space, land-use patterns and local economic development needs clear analysis. Cost-benefit analyses of programmes which have been undertaken should be made public, and the relative success of various incentive programmes and the consideration of alternative approaches require full investigation.

Chapter 2 The Scope of Alternative Physical Planning Systems and their Relationships with Real Estate Markets Internationally

The common law, land-use planning and development

Differing legal systems and conditions give rise to differing property rights and planning regimes in various jurisdictions. The UK, Ireland, Australia, large parts of the US and other parts of the world have both inherited and evolved from a British common law tradition which emphasises individual property rights. Prior to modern planning systems, landowners could resort to common courts which could simply issue injunctions where a property user could be alleged to be impacting on the lawful use and enjoyment of another person's property by causing an adverse external impact, for example, pollution. This could be affected by means of injunctions on use or compensation. In the modern period, multiple competing interests evolved which gave rise to the need for a system of regulation and development control or planning systems.

Many of these jurisdictions have a typology of physical planning operating in a localised manner, with a passive ambit of operations and statutory prescribed planning powers legislated for and a regulatory system based on a development control approach.

This typology of land-use planning with a market-led emphasis has three principal elements: a plan-making function, a developmental function involving issues such as land servicing, and a regulatory or control function. These functions are often carried out in distinct departments of a city, regional, or national authority, leading to fragmentation in both the evidence upon which decisions are based and actual decision-making (Tosics et al., 2010, Williams and Nedović-Budić, 2016).[1]

This tradition of law provides a common basis for the development of citizens' or subjects' rights in all such jurisdictions. The law plays a determining role in the establishment and delineation of property rights and in ensuring the appropriate use of these land rights in conformance with public policy and law. Classic economic theory would argue that this is intended to achieve allocative efficiency, innovation and management of scarce resources by the actions of individual property owners and pricing systems, while a Marxist critique would argue that this ownership system underpins and strengthens existing structural inequalities.

Common law court rulings serve as precedents for similar cases and resolving legal disputes. In effect, legal precedent and a body of law provide a degree of certainty in how disputes are resolved. As voluntary exchange and trade is regarded as beneficial, the law is clearly structured to support such agreements. Trade, voluntary exchanges and adherence to contracts are encouraged. It is beneficial in such systems that property rights are clear and the legal system favours ownership and strong and clear property rights to land and natural resources.

A central feature of this development control-based approach in the UK and other jurisdictions was the introduction of an agreed development plan with statutory backing. National and local policy aspirations are intended to be operationalised via a local development control system grounded on such plans. The introduction of this type of planning in the UK in 1945 represented a democratic and pluralist approach which was used to mediate between national, regional and local policy objectives and development needs. Development proposals are made, and discretion is used by the relevant planning officials or political interests to decide on the merits of individual proposals. Ownership of land was left unchanged and existing uses remained permitted; however, any change of use or proposed development required planning permission or consent to develop.

The role of the courts and legal system was, and is, to ensure that the planning authority has made decisions in accordance with proper procedures in law – *Ultra vires*. Legal consistency and a legal and bureaucratic system have evolved in each jurisdiction, with courts ensuring that relevant material considerations have been used in arriving at decisions. Appeal systems in all the common law planning systems vary, with the rights of third parties or adjacent owners restricted in many jurisdictions. Planning is also subject to public intervention; roles in appeals, including third-party matters to planning authority decisions, vary greatly but are used to achieve consistency in treatment. Discretion and adversarial challenges in such systems leads to tensions which are often ideological.

Land-use zoning is the most commonly used planning instrument, with the regulations stipulating the single or multiple uses of land allowed. Zoning can separate incompatible use such as heavy industrial and related heavy transport use, especially in or near residential areas. With recent modern industry, such as IT companies, there are fewer concerns and there is an increasing use of mixed-use zonings.

Typologies of planning

There are a wide range of international experiences as to how power, in terms of planning physical development, can be centralised or devolved at a local or regional level. The legal style of national systems differs greatly in respect of constitutional and legal rights in respect to property. In addition, the nature of the administrative and political culture of how planning is culturally accepted or not differs globally. Power relationships in urban and regional development decision-making can be genuinely democratic and pluralistic or guided by effective pressure groups and elites or selected interests and coalitions. The scope of national planning styles and systems can range from limited to comprehensive.

Within Europe some jurisdictions have explicit national regional and local plans while others have a purely local development control approach. In a French typology or model, the central government has a dominant, managerial role in national and regional development. Efficient placing of infrastructure is to the fore and a hierarchical approach ensures the integration of national, regional and local planning policies.

A Germanic or Northern European model involves a more comprehensive, integrated approach to planning at all levels of the state. This can involve a high level of coordination of state/public activities and investment with land-use planning. Scandinavian approaches have typically prioritised rational planning approaches to urban development and social inclusion with high levels of public investment. Federal systems such as those in Austria and Germany can involve high levels of coordination between sectors and levels, and require mature administrative systems.

Mediterranean approaches have a high urban design and architectural input, with historic cities governed by complex land use and buildings regulations regarding townscape, place-making and conservation issues, with less attention given to controlling development at the metropolitan or regional scale. This results in an urbanism tradition with a specific focus on historic city quarters.

In the UK, and similar systems following a development control approach, the land-use planning system can be characterised as reliant on indirect development control, in contrast to the direct master planning system more commonly used in continental Europe. It is evident that in such development-led policy systems, the planning process has the advantage of inbuilt flexibility and allows for ongoing negotiation processes between public and private actors. It is also considered, however, that such flexibilities can lead to property speculation and relatively higher prices, and to the more pronounced cyclical trends evident in British property markets compared to other European regions.

In contrast, in other EU continental and international approaches, the land uses as well as the obligations of the landowners and real estate developers are more clearly defined in urban planning documents and policy systems. The continental system can be best illustrated by the post-Second World War

Scandinavian models where the government historically had a direct strategic influence on the urban land market, assisted by spatial planning policies. In general, in these jurisdictions, the urban management and planning system decides which locations will be developed for housing, businesses and infrastructure. A developer must make certain that his plans comply with and do not conflict with the local land-use plan once adopted. If the plans do not conform to the designated use and building regulations, applications for the necessary building permit are refused.

The building permit and land-use plan are powerful instruments for the state sector to structure and selectively guide infrastructure provision and resulting urban development. For example, the German planning systems in the federal states have generally resulted in a less cyclical market than many other European markets. Historically, the German property market has been characterised by a high level of supply to meet demand and moderate rental and price growth.

The seminal EU Compendium of Spatial Planning Systems and Policies project (1997)[2] defined spatial planning as a combination of land-use regulation and the coordination of the territorial impacts of sector policies. Since then, spatial planning has been used more often to describe the national systems of land-use planning, while the notion of territorial governance has evolved to describe the role of planning in coordinating sector policies. The working definitions adopted in the European Union ESPON/Compass project (2018)[3] give a suitable platform for a discussion of alternative planning systems:

> Territorial governance comprises the institutions that assist in active cooperation across government, market and civil society actors to coordinate decision-making and actions that have an impact on the quality of places and their development. Spatial planning systems are the ensemble of institutions that are used to mediate competition over the use of land and property, to allocate rights of development, to regulate change and to promote preferred spatial and urban form.

This report on planning systems in 32 European countries found that the 32 countries included in the survey used, in total, 255 different types of planning instrument. The instruments often had a mix of functions including visionary, strategic, framework and regulative types. Strategic functions tend to dominate at the national level and the regulative function at the local level, and many planning instruments fulfil multiple functions.

National planning instruments across the EU have evolved from 2000 to the present date with a consistency in the changes to the plan and permit procedures which mostly involve simplification and/or streamlining of procedures, adapting to digital technology and strengthening regulation and reasoning in decision-making. There is also a trend towards more transparency and citizen engagement in the planning process. There are specific objectives for reform including regularising informal or illegal development and introducing more value capture or planning gain from development.

Market approaches to planning in the US

In the US, a written constitution protects the right to private property and courts may take cautious positions on regulatory interference. Under this interpretation of common law, the owner retains the right to develop lands provided she/he does not adversely affect the property rights of others. Many states in the US have adopted planning systems with characteristics such as zoning and development control consistent with similar systems in Europe and globally. However, within the federal system it also provides examples of systems and approaches which provide alternatives for consideration.

As an alternative to planning/zoning, private markets can also evolve systems which allow for voluntary or cooperative sharing of development rights in a land-use planning context. This can include voluntary agreements, with negotiated agreements involving easements over land, covenants or restrictions on use and transferable development rights. Where investment in land development is pursued, these agreements can substitute for land use planning, with Houston, Texas often cited as an example.

Experimentation with market-based planning systems has been seen in the US where it provides a means of compensating landowners for trading away their development rights without regulatory expropriation of such tradeable development rights (TDR). The initial allocation of such rights is often still subject to a regulatory limitation in terms of quantity of development.

Examples of TDR have been developed in the states of New Jersey and California. Under such a system, areas can be specified as development zones or conservation zones, but critically development rights are allocated to landowners in all zones. The rights to development can be sold but development is permitted only in development zones, in a system intended to facilitate transfers of rights and higher densities to such areas.

Shahab et al. (2018)[4] contend that planners could implement these programmes as an alternative to traditional regulatory instruments, such as zoning, subdivision regulations and purchase of development rights (PDR) programmes. Local governments can use PDR programmes to purchase development rights in preservation areas using public funds. TDR programmes, in contrast, do not use public funds and instead let the development market pay to preserve land by purchasing development rights from lands within designated areas. The TDR approach is like zoning: public sector planners recommend which areas to develop and to preserve, as illustrated in Figure 5. TDR programmes use market mechanisms, rather than traditional regulatory instruments, to achieve greater efficiency, allowing development rights to be traded between landowners who wish to engage in the development process in a regulated market process.

As of 2016, US local governments operated 254 TDR programmes in 36 states, most dating from the 1980s. TDR programmes establish markets to trade and transfer development rights translated into TDR credits between different areas, which allows planners to protect lands they would otherwise need to buy. Landowners in 'sending areas' may sell development rights, calculated as TDR credits, at prices set by the market. Developers may purchase and use those credits in 'receiving areas', which planners designate for development. The original landowners maintain the property rights but forgo the development rights in perpetuity after selling them. TDR programmes normally provide developers with an option to obtain extra density (bonus density) to develop beyond a specific permitted level in 'receiving areas'. This also allows for protection of sensitive lands, reducing preservation costs for local governments.

TDR programmes can be an alternative to traditional instruments such as zoning, in which large benefits are conferred on those fortunate enough to be zoned for development, but there is no transfer of funds to compensate those whose land is zoned for preservation.

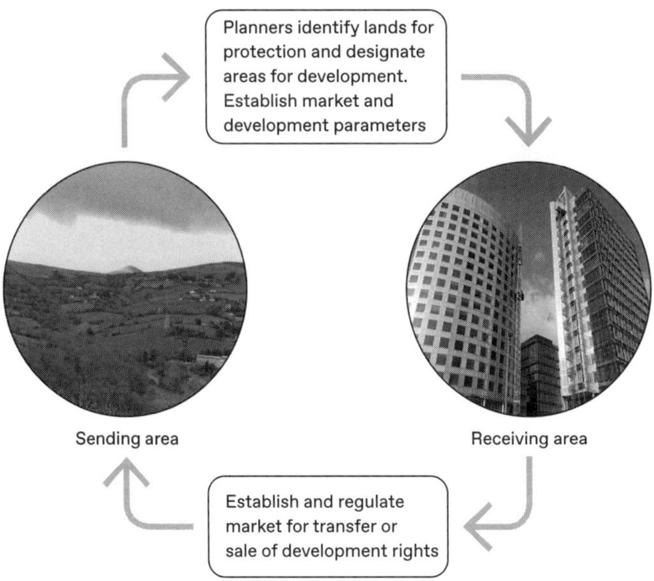

Figure 5
Transferring development rights credits from sending areas to receiving areas

Further international comparisons of planning and real estate interactions

The challenges faced by each land-use planning system are similar, but the effects of land-use planning can only be fully understood in the context of each country's land-use planning and real estate interactions. Changes in use and new development are required for the changing demands of every modern society, both within existing urban areas and on greenfield land which requires new infrastructure, including electricity, water, schools, health facilities and road and rail links. Examples of the more comprehensive land-use planning exist where larger scale land-use plans integrate the development of infrastructure, natural resources, recreational and environmental issues, including the Netherlands and parts of Asia (Brandt, 2014).[5] In these cases, developers are required to contribute directly to infrastructure open space, etc., in their development projects.

Broader approaches to comprehensive planning integrated in policy-making include the historic importance of land-use planning – in the Netherlands due to the inherent dangers of flooding on populated reclaimed lands – through to the examples of corporatism or partnership in late-twentieth-century Germany, where the process of policy-making is formulated between employers, employees and state inputs (Abraham, 2017).[6] Examples include the integrated planning approach to the supported transition of the Ruhr area of North Rhine-Westphalia, Germany to bring about the ending of subsidised hard coal mining by 2018. This has involved major public investment in infrastructure, education and housing. This type of proactive planning – improving transport links, ensuring environmental improvements in what were heavily polluted areas and planning new physical and economic development – has been assisted by local, regional and national governments. The engagement of national government is essential in such programmes, as economic restructuring and transitions can obviously have a negative impact on local municipal budgets. The result of such policies is clear, both in the ongoing physical renewal of the Ruhr area, and in cities and training programmes to create a shift towards new business and technologies, often located in modern, green energy sectors.

Planning and real estate – treatment of development gains

Development gains can be defined as the increase in land prices related directly to changes in planning regulations and are of critical interest to landowners, developers and planners. For example, lands used for agriculture adjacent to an urban area may be priced at £10–20,000 per acre, whereas the same lands – if zoned for housing – might achieve £200,000 per acre and upwards.

Land-use planning tries to balance the interests of landowners and the wider concerns of public policy and society. Therefore, the creation of windfall gains through changes in the development plan, and limitations on numbers of specific projects, for example, office parks or shopping centres, confers monopoly values on permitted developments, creating super-normal profits, and is problematic. Some argue that market-led development planning permissions should be simply sold to the highest bidder or opened up to invited tenders, which could assess both the bid price and the qualities of development proposed. Proponents of such alternative approaches question whether planning is efficient or if the regulation of land use is producing effective policy outcomes. This debate questions if, under private market operations, land ownership and exposure to competition could allocate resources more efficiently. Regarding development gains, liberal economics and property industry interests argue that such recoupment should happen through normal taxation processes such as income tax, corporation tax and capital gains taxes.

Lands not favoured or zoned for development can still retain – in real estate agency terms – 'hope value', which is an expectation that in a subsequent development plan – whether by lobbying, the natural growth of an urban area or other means – the lands become deemed suitable for development. This creates in effect a permanent process of speculation and trading in land markets on both existing planning consents and the future possibilities of consent to develop.

The OECD (2017)[7] reported that across the developed world there is a need to plan and provide adequate supplies of land to supply affordable housing and built developments in areas well connected with transport and required infrastructure, while internalising or minimising externalities such as air pollution and congestion. The high costs of both real estate development and the associated public resources and developments which are provided to support such development needs planners, public policy-makers and real estate developers to cooperate in each jurisdiction.

A critical issue for this analysis is that of development costs, betterment or planning gain, whereby real estate interests, community interests and planners either share or do not share the associated costs and benefits of such development. Recovering some of these costs can be achieved by development levies, where the cost is contributed to by the developers and the purchasers of built space, or more by widely using property taxes or general taxation. The wide range of approaches to land value capture mechanisms internationally is shown in Table 2.

Externalities (costs affecting a third party and not reflected in the market price) of the development of land include the provision of infrastructure needs, schools and public facilities. From an environmental perspective, the loss of open space, congestion, air pollution and construction disruption are additional costs. Failure to cost and properly integrate externalities in the development can contribute to expansions of urban areas at low densities with segregated land uses and limited infrastructure provision. These are often not considered or internalised into land-use development decisions and contribute to poor, inefficient land use such as urban sprawl.

In the US, levies or development cost charges have been used as a means of recovering local infrastructure costs by way of a once-off fee. Development impact fees to cover the cost of infrastructure needed by new housing are commonly used

Table 2
Land value capture mechanisms

Impact Fees	Joint Develop-ments	Property Tax (only for countries that update tax-base regularly)	Land Banking/ Pre-Emptive Purchase Rights at Unimproved Valuations	Tax Increment Financing	Betterment Levy	No Value Capture
Australia	Austria	Australia	Austria	Canada	Israel	Belgium
Austria	Czech Republic	Chile	Finland	Finland	Poland	Hungary
Estonia	Denmark	Denmark	Germany	France	United States	Ireland
Finland	Estonia	Finland	Japan	Korea		Slovenia
France	Finland	Japan	Korea	Spain		United Kingdom
Germany	Israel	Korea	Norway	United States		
Greece	Japan	Mexico	Spain			
Israel	Korea	New Zealand	United States			
Italy	Mexico	Portugal				
Japan	Netherlands	Turkey				
Korea	New Zealand	United States				
Netherlands	Norway					
New Zealand	Slovak Republic					
Slovak Republic	Switzerland					
Sweden	United States					
Switzerland						
United States						
17	15	11	8	6	3	5

in parts of the US. Brueckner and Saavedra (2001)[8] present the positive impacts of these fees in ensuring developers internalise infrastructure costs which may assist in reviving decaying inner areas which require less new infrastructure. In Canada, impact fees have been used in Ontario to cover the cost of providing public infrastructure such as public utilities, roads, etc., and external costs associated with the development proposed by development levies. If transferred to new home purchasers, this can result in both increased house prices and decreases in development land values.

In a development-led system such as the UK, Corkingdale (1999)[9] argued that in the 1945 Acts the state had effectively nationalised land development rights and gave planning authorities the power to privatise those rights on a partial and discretionary basis. Developers were originally to pay a development charge amounting to 100 per cent of the increase in the value of lands resulting from any subsequent development and the development charge or tax was to be accompanied by a compensation system for development rights nationalised. The development charge and fund were abolished by the incoming Conservative government in 1953. A subsequent development charge was introduced at a level of 40 per cent by an incoming Labour government in 1967 and abolished by a Conservative government in 1971; the development charges introduced by Labour in 1976 were amended and abolished by 1985. This critical linkage between planning and development process which underpinned the introduction of planning has never been resolved in later policy implementation and remains contested in political and ideological debates.

Planning obligations associated with planning consent replaced planning gain in 1991. With the Great Financial Crisis (GFC) many such agreements collapsed and companies in liquidation could not provide the obligations promised. Due to the lack of transparency in negotiations, these approaches are sometimes criticised as an example of a planning system being used for tax-raising purposes, with allegations of local political corruption with deals made in smoke-filled rooms. There is often public confusion as to the true purpose of planning agreements, along with other categories of public and private developments, and concern as to whether they best serve long-term policy objectives.

Property taxation of real estate and planning

Tax breaks or exemptions to groups/activities can be used to promote desirable planning and real estate outcomes. Property tax relief was used widely in modern urban housing development to promote owner occupation by subsidised mortgage schemes and urban regeneration, starting with the US in the 1940s, while more recent examples of tax-based initiatives internationally promote investments in property-related renewable energy. In effect, subsidies are used with property taxation measures applied to influence land use through changing the costs or incentives to build, develop or leave land vacant and undeveloped, such as disused brownfield or former industrial lands.

There have been continuous international policy debates since the nineteenth century on the potential benefits of a pure land tax. In political debates of the early twentieth century, contributors – for example, the land theorist Henry George (1879) in the US, and Winston Churchill – have recognised that land is effectively fixed in supply terms which cannot be changed by the introduction of a land tax (Brandt, 2014).[10] While the base supply of land is fixed, it is of course affected by planning regulations including densities, height controls, etc. The central argument remains that changes in land value driven by land-use planning in present systems are often windfall gains and should be taxed (Barker, 2004),[11] and this also raises the difficult policy question: should the losses incurred by other landowners also be compensated under the present system?

However, the behaviour of landowners may be altered in that land rents are seen to be determined by location and public action, such as zoning and infrastructure development, rather than by the individual landowners' efforts. The logical policy progression is that it is fair and equitable to at least tax these rents to finance the provision of public services and influence development decisions.

Vacant and brownfield lands can have significant negative effects on the surrounding area including underuse of existing infrastructure. Instead, development at such sites can contribute to shorter commutes and easier public transport demand, with greater use of passive transport types including walking and cycling.

Taxes on land could reduce the incentive for landowners to apply for planning permission, except in cases where there is a definite intention to develop, rather than enhance land value by obtaining favourable planning conditions for future development. Muellbauer (2005)[12] argues that a tax on land values also has the potential to limit housing price bubbles, as the share of the tax in imputed rents and incomes should rise when land prices rise faster than imputed rents. Therefore, land taxes can be largely neutral in terms of investment and development but would increase the cost of holding land. Central areas with higher land values and corresponding potential land taxes should be developed sooner, and withholding and speculation in land should be disincentivised.

Property transaction taxes or stamp duties are common in many common law countries and seem to be politically acceptable as a policy option. They are, however, seen to hinder both mobility and reallocation of buildings and land as they may discourage or delay transactions. Their effect can be to encourage the incentive to buy cheap land further away from centres and build new buildings, which generally attracts lower or no transaction costs. The boost to new build and unintended taxation distortions can discourage the purchase and refurbishment of existing properties.

The OECD notes that programmes need to be analysed in country-specific contexts. Reforms in Germany suggest differential land taxes based on use, and in Switzerland, new land planning law foresees a tax on planning-induced value increases and planning-induced value losses being compensated.

Planning and real estate – housing

As housing is often the sector from which we approach the interactions of planning and real estate interests, we may examine alternative policy approaches to housing provision and the wider lessons for planning processes. This range of approaches includes options from a light touch regulation/development control approach to a highly integrated approach. At opposite ends of the spectrum might be the historically integrated approach to social housing as a concept in Austria and Germany, compared to the housing of lower socio-economic groups/ethnic groups in single socio-economic estates in public provision and market provision for higher income groups in a neo-liberal context.

Planning and housing policy in Sweden, Denmark, Switzerland and Austria evolved based on an integrated approach to housing, with a unitary housing system or markets without regulatory barriers between profit and non-profit providers. Kemeny (2005, 2006)[13] argues that 50 years of maturation was involved in such systems attempting to avoid extremes of laissez-faire and command economy approaches. Strong non-profit sectors evolved, housing residents of mixed incomes and often charging cost-based rents which were lower than market rents with long-term leasing arrangements. This could be termed a social market model with a significant non-profit sector, often equal in size to the private sector, as in Vienna. Such systems also feature strong tenant protection and tenant responsibilities, along with regulated rents and leasing terms. Recent responses to the homeless problem again illustrate differences in responses, with Finland adopting a directed *housing provision first* response to the issue and many other jurisdictions reliant on charitable agencies supported by public funds to indirectly address the issue.

Alternatively, the recent UK, Irish and US experiences are dominated by a dualist market approach. This involves the residual lower income and means-tested sections of demand being catered for by public agencies, while the principal housing supply process for the larger private market is delivered by the private sector, aided by incentives and tax breaks such as mortgage relief.

Planning in this system treats housing largely as a private market commodity to be provided and bought/invested in, with the state intervening mainly to address demand from the residual low-income sectors. In such systems the public or social housing sector is often diminished over time. Occupiers of social housing were initially offered options of purchase – after time periods and other conditions – under rental purchase schemes. This was followed by a strong policy approach favouring the disposal process, with many 'Right to Buy' schemes reducing the stock of social housing. Following sale of social housing stock, the state now encourages housing associations to produce for individual market sectors such as the elderly, etc. It can be argued that a multi-pronged policy push to advance home ownership, followed by a response to the financial crisis, which aimed to refloat both banks and all asset classes by quantitative easing, has significantly contributed to a widespread, affordable housing crisis. This involved a response to solving a financial crisis compounding and exacerbating an affordable housing problem.

Responding to the financial crisis of 2008–2009, major central banks, including the US Federal Reserve and the Bank of England, began asset purchase programmes to stabilise the financial system and stimulate economic growth. Within the Euro system, national central banks bought tranches of assets from banks to help stimulate the economy. Central banks use quantitative easing, a tool that in the Euro area is called the expanded Asset Purchase Programme (APP). This increases the price of these assets and creates additional quantities of money in the banking system and economy. In addition, with the adoption of low interest rates, loans become cheaper and businesses and individuals can borrow more and spend less to repay their existing and new debts. As a result, consumption and investment receive a boost, driving higher consumption and more investment, in turn supporting economic growth, job creation and asset price recovery and inflation.

This resulted in a sharp recovery in banking and asset classes, including property. These policies were allied with a simultaneous reduction in public spending and real salary levels reducing available real household incomes. This combination of rapid increasing in asset values and housing prices with slower or no growth in household income levels has contributed to a housing affordability crisis which is global in scale.

In many ways the result of the emergency rescue of the financial system over the last decade illustrates the deep and complex relationships which have evolved between financial, political, property and planning policy interests. Managing such relationships in a market-led planning environment presents significant challenges to all the parties involved and necessitates an examination and appreciation of the economic and property context shaping all development decisions in a market economy.

Chapter 3 Development-led Systems and the Pivotal Role of Real Estate Interests

Objectives of public and private interests

Money matters and financial issues have a decisive role in most planning and development decisions, which invariably create tensions and new distributions of winners and losers. Real estate and development interests wish to optimise land use at individual locations and maximise profits. This often does not consider the costs and effects of new development on the wider public and can differ from planners' wishes to achieve the objectives of their development plan without their own resources to achieve implementation. The reality of this situation is that development profit is the area in which the essential trade-off of the private market wishes and the planner's objectives occurs. An understanding of the development decision-making process can assist in shaping potential means of integrating such activity into broader policy aims.

Development profit at a specific site is normally the single focus of market development activity. However, the sum of those development decisions represents a major power in directing patterns of urban development. An understanding of the role of the developer in the property market and his or her decision-making process thereby enhances planning and policy initiatives in the property development context, whether in terms of development planning and regulation, urban renewal or public/private partnership arrangements. In this chapter, the primary relationship between prices, costs, valuation assessments and supply are illustrated in a series of simplified development appraisals, highlighting the influence of planning decisions. This will include the general influence of planning controls on prices, along with critical inputs subject to planning control, such as densities.

Development appraisal decisions reflect analysis by property market participants in the development process of future movement in supply and demand, finance and construction capital. Decisions made, and the interplay of these forces, can create substantial risk in decisions involving the physical process of production of buildings within an uncertain social economic and political context. An analysis of the property development decision process, and its sequence of evaluations on markets and activities, is therefore essential to an understanding of the high level of risk and return involved.

Many planning gain/sharing arrangements, land disposals and public/private partnerships are ultimately based on appraisal decisions. In effect, the planning or public agency partners in such arrangements often negotiate favourable planning consents or trade land at less than open market value for varying levels of required developments or services to be provided by competing/bidding private sector interests. Negotiating arrangements with a land development component can be a complex process involving estimates and assessments of future market trends.

Assessing the feasibility or profitability of development options is a key element in all development decisions. The residual approach or method is normally used in valuation of property where latent development value is the prime determinant of overall valuation assessment. Categories of land where this approach might be used include sites for development, refurbishment of buildings and other property situations, where a future potential use value is greater than the value based upon the present use. The basis of such decisions is that the market is likely to link the potential future value of the property to the decision to purchase and initiate development. The key question then becomes whether the surplus or profit which can be generated by the potential development is enough to justify the risk involved. An outline of this type of appraisal involves the estimation of the development value of various alternative projects at the location and a comparison of this value with the costs of achieving development.

Fundamental to this approach is a knowledge of recent market transactions for sites with similar development possibilities. This can indicate a range of potential prices for the locality, along with evidence of sales and rental levels of completed units for comparison purposes. The unique physical location and other attributes of each site necessitate an individual valuation approach. In this way, it is then possible to carry out an analysis of options, such as establishing a potential sale value of a development site, determining the feasibility of various development options or establishing the optimum intensity or quality of a proposed development.

While this approach is primarily associated with speculative development decisions, the basic elements of the appraisal approach are similar for a wide spectrum of potential decision-makers involved in the process, and could include a diverse range of participants, including examples as can be seen in Figure 6.

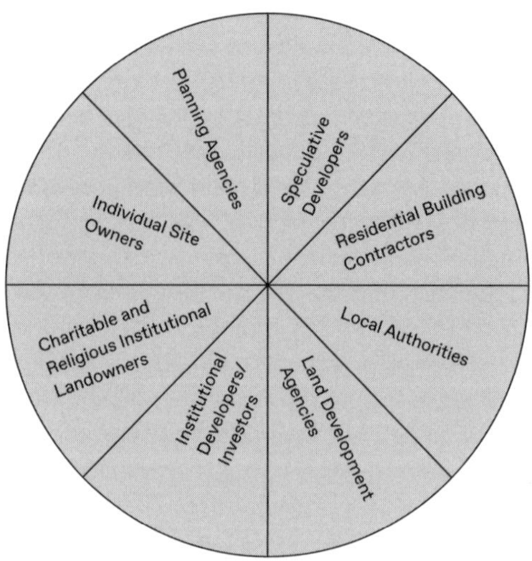

Figure 6
Potential decision-makers in the development process

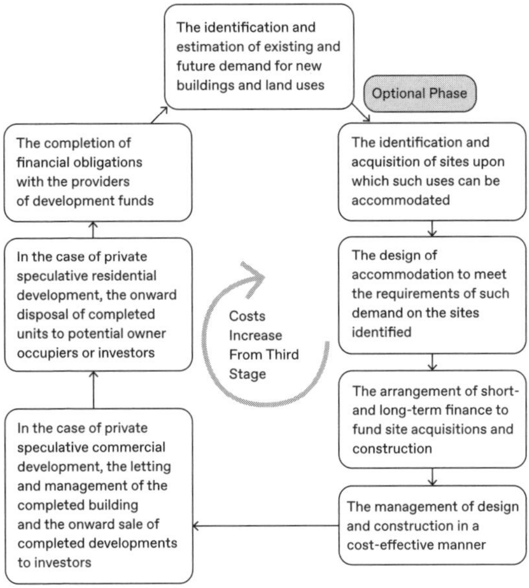

Figure 7
The appraisal and decision-making process, showing the increase in costs as the process progresses

The next issue for consideration is the varying objectives of the various interests in the development process. While profit optimisation, seeking the highest-value use and financial return, is the obvious starting objective of private market interests, the containment and minimisation of risk is also an objective of a prudent market participant. For public sector participants, specific issues such as providing affordable accommodation and achieving community or public resource goals may dominate, depending on the site and current priorities in policy.

To understand how both public and private sectors negotiate and determine such arrangements, it is necessary to review and appreciate the essential elements of appraisal and decision-making in the property development process regarding a specific development site. These can involve the completion of the processes shown in Figure 7.

All estimates and evaluations are carried out subject to competition at all levels, which plays a major role in the culture of the property development industry. Specialist companies, which have evolved from speculative building concerns, are what would customarily be regarded as property developers. These interests can be involved in regional, national and international markets using market and non-market experience and knowledge to evaluate and test development projects. This involves analysis of demand in uncertain and imperfect markets, along with the state of current supply and the proposals of other development interests to supply this market. Each stage of the process is costly and time-consuming, and involves decisions based upon analysis of risk. As the building design is agreed and capital is committed, heavy costs are incurred.

Development of a project

Once a site is purchased or capital committed, interest payments commence immediately. Risks of unforeseen expenditures increase during the construction phase. It is at the later stages following fitting out that major risk is involved. Instead of an option on a site or ownership of a piece of development land with many possible uses, the developer now has a partially finished product. This product is fixed at a specific location, its future economic and market context when completed is out of the developer's control. Many developments are for sale as investments on an open market which can be volatile and unpredictable. In this context, the public sector development element of a public/private partnership must be guaranteed and needs to be covered by the profitability of the remaining components.

In such situations, the developer and other participants are faced with the most difficult area of uncertainty: that of timing, as developments will often take more than two years from initiation to completion. The determination of accurate assessments of costs and expenditures throughout the project development period presents major problems and detailed forecasting is needed for feasibility studies. However, these may be, and remain, only estimates based on incomplete knowledge. Changes in the property market and other economic cycles present different scenarios and problems for all decision-makers. Cyclical development patterns often involve developments being completed during periods of oversupply in the market. Development interests can therefore, at no stage, avoid risks, but different approaches can be taken to potential risks based on information, analysis and forecasts.

Property development interests

Because of the capital borrowing requirements of the participants in the development process, a deeper involvement of the larger financial institutions has evolved over recent decades. Until the 1960s, these institutions were primarily involved as providers of mortgages and finance on development property and as investors in completed projects. Exposure of investments and loans to property market corrections and slumps highlighted the burden of high risk associated with property investment and loans. In a downturn, property companies are forced into liquidation and default on repaying loans, which contrasts strongly with the disproportionate high returns enjoyed by developers during previous booms based on low or fixed interest loans.

An increased involvement in the development market saw institutions initially taking stakes in developments while later becoming involved as developers. Institutional developers will often be acting with an investment interest in view, with the parent company (for example, a life assurance or pension fund group) retaining the completed development for rental and capital growth. Otherwise, where developments are for onward sale, the attitude and decision-making of the institutions would resemble that of the main property development companies.

The remaining property development interests include both existing occupiers and owners along with public sector agencies. Occupiers, and particularly owner-occupiers, are involved in maximising the use and potential of their existing location. Risk-taking for development by such participants is normally at a lower level than for speculative development.

The bulk of development activity by occupiers and owners is for their own use and consequently their return is by way of their use of the property. This is assessed based on the extra profit which can be derived from expenditure based on inputs, including known levels of business and costs. When owner-occupiers expand the scale of their development beyond their own known requirements, they enter the area of speculative development, with similar risks to those of conventional speculative development situations.

The role of the public sector in providing development is substantially different from the other interests, whether direct provision, or by means of partnerships. Social and economic considerations are included in the public service analysis of developments. Such analysis would essentially involve the political consideration of social needs allied with evaluation of cost/benefit analysis as to the efficient use of scarce public sector funds. Where public sector agencies combine with private sector interests, the negotiations by the private interest will revolve around conventional development appraisal assessments of profitability conditioned by the requirements of the public agency included as a cost on the development. This cost is of course normally balanced by the availability of land at a lower than normal price in exchange. However, both sides need accurate development appraisal estimates to negotiate successfully.

In terms of the general bidding process for development land, competition between property developers, owners and the public sector involves the payment of high prices for suitable development sites. In an active market, potential purchasers compete for the limited suitable development land on the market. While developers will attempt at all stages to minimise costs and risks involved, land purchase decisions involve upward price movement due to competing bids. Land purchase and financing of development brings the developer into negotiations with the other capital interests in the process – land, finance and investment providers – as to shares in the eventual return accruing from the potential property development.

Negotiations on land purchase price, financing or equity sharing arrangements and onward sale arrangements dictate the level of return to the development company and all other participants. Although it may be possible to contract out some of the essential elements of the process, the final risk is borne by the developer and the provider or guarantor of finance. A similar process can evolve as development interests compete for valuable sites which are the subject of a bidding process for public/private development projects. Several groups may compete and offer various financial packages as a return to a public agency or private interest owning land for development. Joint ventures or consortiums are often created for a development project with the use of special purpose vehicles which are incorporated companies established by another trading company, individuals or private investors for the sole purpose of that development. The negotiations of such arrangements are based on risk and return calculations by each participant. Distribution of returns in such situations is decided by negotiations between the landowner, development and finance providers based on cost inputs and returns expected. Various models exist for each potential consortium or joint venture and are represented in Figure 8.

In the first model – horizontal sharing – some or all the participants are seeking a fixed share or amount of the resulting revenue prior to the development being completed. This analysis will be based on their analysis of the development and the viability or profit expected from the development. A fixed or guaranteed ground rent to a landowner or guaranteed bottom slice can be used by such participants to minimise risk. A top slice, going to perhaps the landowner, carries risk if the market for the development is not as strong as expected on completion.

In the next model – vertical sharing – all parties share the risk of the development equally, taking part shares of whatever development value or rental value results in the completed development.

The last model represents a mix of vertical and horizontal sharing arrangements, with one or more parties seeking a fixed

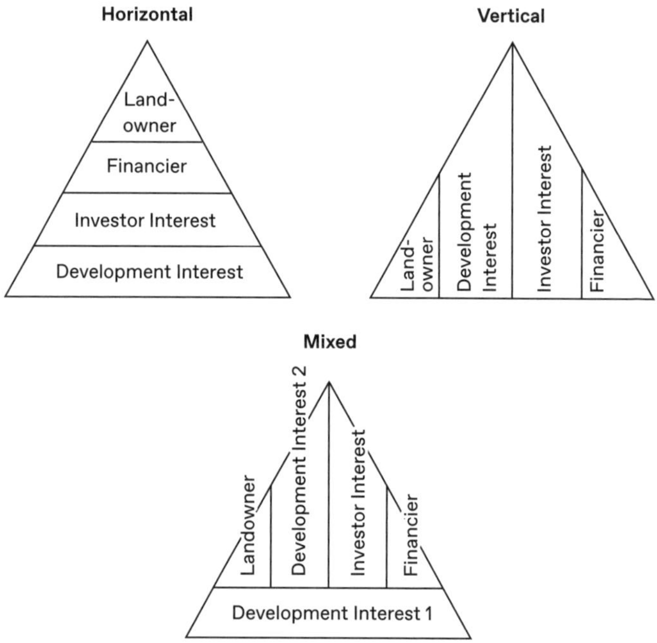

Figure 8
Horizontal, vertical and linked arrangements

return and other participants bearing both a greater risk but also perhaps a greater return if development values are greater than expected.

Decision-making often leads to specialisation in a given sector or market niche and is an obvious route to survival and success in highly competitive situations. The capability of companies to participate in major developments during cyclical upswings, when rents, returns and investor demand are high, has considerable effects on output in these sectors. The tendency toward occasional boom and slump conditions, particularly within the commercial office sector, is much in evidence.

Similarly, specialisation can occur by concentrating on one part of the development process, with some companies active only in on-site identification, acquisition and onward sale of lands with planning permission to other developers. Such development interests have emerged specialising in land acquisition and assembly, both requiring considerable time and management. Other development/planning specialists will attempt to create added value by achieving outline or full planning permission, which competitors might not foresee or achieve, requiring high-risk site acquisition and considerable management skills. Finally, in certain enterprise zones or tax concession-designated areas, the taxation specialist has become established as the individual who packages both development and investment processes, maximising such advantages. Involvement in this area requires an understanding of taxation and incentive systems to maximise the total return from any property development using all allowances, including the cost of borrowing. Companies can also establish strategies in terms of both geographical spread and market sectors to minimise the risk of over-exposure to a single market or sector.

Investigation of property development companies and their employment of varying strategies to ensure company efficiency indicates some features of good long-term management and can include:

1 Ensuring the cost of investment on projects is kept to a minimum by favourable funding arrangements.
2 Close monitoring and control of construction phases in developments.
3 Achieving a high degree of pre-lettings or pre-sales on favourable terms prior to commencement through being aware of clients' needs and forging relationships with clients, estate agents and other parties in the sector.

The development industry functions basically as the facilitator of present and future demand requirements of both the investors and consumers of built space. The demand for buildings is a derived demand resulting from the real

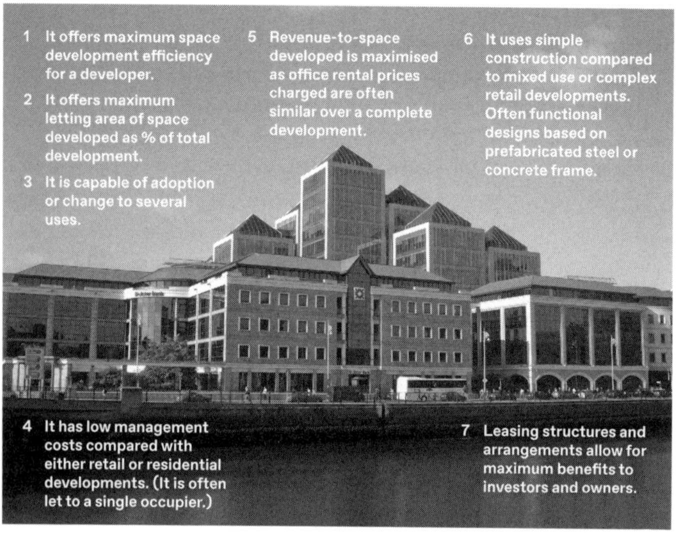

Figure 9
Investor office sector preference

economy and structural changes within that economy, which continually result in changes in demand for space. The property development industry, therefore, is attempting to satisfy present and future demand and derive profits from the process.

Profitability and future expectations of profits are therefore the key issues in development trends. A rising market with increased demand produces increasing rents, values and profits. Within a private market, land will tend to its most profitable use. Therefore, prime sites enjoying maximum accessibility, convenience and suitability to alternative uses will tend to be occupied by the highest bidders. New office development remains the highest value use in locations such as central business districts, for the reasons illustrated in Figure 9.

In terms of urban locations, developers have preferred, historically, commercial development in central business districts and lower density residential development at green field locations. Medium density residential development at central urban locations has been the norm in many parts of continental Europe; planning policies have encouraged residential development at higher densities in central redevelopment sites from the 1990s to date in the UK and Ireland.

Developers were initially reluctant to switch to residential development where design and density criteria are radically different to traditional suburban housing. Security, servicing and maintenance of common areas are all more problematical issues within the management of residential development projects. Obviously, the development of a large, high-density residential project with entirely different marketing, financing and project management requirements is not the preferred option of some development companies. However, problems of office cycles and oversupply have increasingly led to a switch in emphasis to residential development. With cost-effective building methods and smaller units, it has become possible to develop residential apartments at central locations at profitable prices. The trend towards development in this sector is in line with sustainable planning objectives of compact urban form and prioritising the redevelopment of brown field sites.

Development appraisal and assessing market options

Approaches grounded in the residual method of development appraisal have been the preferred approach to evaluating development proposals within the property industry and professions in many parts of the developed world. In the UK, the Royal Institution of Chartered Surveyors provides guidance as to valuation principles and concepts whereby the appraiser/ valuer brings together the various cost and revenue factors and, having established the completed value, subtracts all development costs to determine the estimated land value for that proposed development. This estimate identifies the maximum price that can be paid for a site to achieve a fixed profit based on expected costs and returns. The development appraisal process can involve researching constraints and opportunities for potential development sites and includes revenue and costs pricing estimates considering market considerations of the location, legal issues, planning aspects and physical characteristics (RICS, 2019).[1] This process is widely used by development interests.

In the UK the Homes and Communities Agency (HCA) suggests that development appraisal provides an approach or tool to assess development viability for planning, which has become an important issue for many local authorities and their partners. Uses suggested in planning include for work on the Community Infrastructure Levy and the 2015–2018 Affordable Homes Programme Framework which impact on development viability (HCA, 2019).[2]

The HCA Development Appraisal Tool (DAT) provides a site-specific development viability tool that is freely available to any user and is designed to inform the development management process by appraising the viability of specific sites. Suggested uses of the tool include:

- Analysis of a scheme when considering whether the level of required planning obligations is viable.
- Helping a local authority consider the balance between affordable housing and other planning obligations.
- Assessing the case for financial support from the HCA under the Affordable Homes Programme.
- Assessment of the potential land value where a local authority is considering a disposal. Individual local authorities and agencies have also adapted this approach towards their own use.

(Trafford City Council, 2019)[3]

If land costs are already known, land cost is included as a development cost and the residual value is the difference between total revenues and costs available for developer's profit. A further conventional use of this approach is such that, where land cost and developer's profit are already established, the method can be used to establish a construction cost maximum with contingencies for the project to remain profitable. With the advent of spreadsheets and software packages, the simple residual approach has been adapted to allow for the phasing of development projects and the detailed calculations of periodic cash flows on projects, as illustrated in the following examples. (See the brief description of technical terms used at the end of this chapter.)

As a first step we consider the position of a commercial developer who has paid £1,000,000 for a plot of land which has planning permission to build a retail distribution centre with offices of total gross size 3,000m^2. Rents of £100 per m^2 overall are the market norm in the vicinity for similar modern buildings. Initial yields or returns in the region of 5 per cent are reported for similar properties, meaning that investors are paying up to twenty times the initial rent to purchase such assets (in the property industry the term '20 YP' – or '20 years purchase' – is used). Construction costs are estimated at £700 per m^2. Finance can be arranged at a cost of £300,000 and the development is likely to take approximately 18 months to complete and let.

This approach gives a clear indication of whether this proposal is financially viable. However, a criticism of this approach is that it is fundamentally based on a single point in time analysis. Given the cycles in each market sector, it is logical that at least this should be supplemented by a range of assessments including a range of optimistic and pessimistic scenarios as to rents and other principal inputs. In particular it can be argued that in the commercial and housing markets, for example, many regions have displayed significant volatility, with both major price increases and corrections in recent years. In the second example we explore how such volatility might be assessed in a housing development project. The following example and table on inputs from a development appraisal indicate how such uncertainty can be analysed. Here, the best and worst outcomes which are expected are inputted and their impact on the outcome assessed.

I. Commercial development appraisal

A. Gross development value (GDV)	£	£
Rental income at £100 per m^2 for 3,000 m^2	300,000	
YP in perp at 5%	20	
Gross development value	6,000,000	
B. Development costs (DC)		
Building costs at £700 per m^2 for 4,000 m^2	2,800,000	
Professional fees	300,000	
Finance cost	300,000	
Letting at 10% of rent	30,000	
Land	1,000,000	
Acquisition cost	50,000	
Total development cost	4,480,000	
C. Development profit= A-B		
available in 18 months	1,520,000	
Profit on development cost =	1,520,000 on DC	4,480,000 = 33.9%
Profit as a return on Gross Development Value =	1,520,000 on GDV	6,000,000 = 25.3%

II. Optimistic scenario valuation

A. Gross development value (GDV)	£	£
Rental income at £110 per m^2 for 3,000 m^2	330,000	
YP in perp at 5%	20	
Gross development value	6,600,000	
B. Development costs (DC)		
Building costs at £700 per m^2 for 4,000 m^2	2,800,000	
Professional fees	300,000	
Finance cost	300,000	
Letting at 10% of rent	33,000	
Land	1,000,000	

Acquisition cost	50,000	
Total development cost	4,483,000	
C. Development profit		
available in 18 months	2,117,000	
Profit on development cost =	2,117,000 on DC	4,483,000 = 47.2%
Profit as a return on Gross Development Value =	2,117,000 on GDV	6,600,000 = 32.1%

III. Pessimistic scenario valuation

A. Gross development value (GDV)	£	£
Rental income at £90 per m^2 for 3,000 m^2	270,000	
YP in perp at 5%	20	
Gross development value	5,400,000	
B. Development costs (DC)		
Building costs at £700 per m^2 for 4,000 m^2	2,800,000	
Professional fees	300,000	
Finance cost	300,000	
Letting at 10% of rent	27,000	
Land	1,000,000	
Acquisition cost	50,000	
Total development cost	4,470,000	
C. Development profit		
available in 18 months	923,000	
Profit on development cost =	923,000 on DC	4,470,000 = 20.9%
Profit as a return on Gross Development Value =	923,000 on GDV	5,400,000 = 17.3%

In the following example a freehold interest in a cleared site has planning approval for the construction of 50 detached houses and the development period is estimated at two years. The expected sale price of the houses is set at £350,000 each. Construction costs are estimated at £145,000 per housing unit and the cost of site works and the provision of services is assessed at an average of £15,500 per house site or plot. Finance has been arranged costing £18,000 per unit, and a developer's profit of 15 per cent on the gross development value of completed units is considered acceptable. A development appraisal or residual valuation can be conducted as follows.

Abbreviated residential development appraisal £/€

Gross Development Value (GDV)	
Sale price of housing units	350,000
Development cost per unit (DC)	
Building costs	145,000
Site works and services	15,500
Professional fees at 10%	35,000
Advertising	4,000
Finance cost arranged	18,000
Disposal fees at 3% of sale price	10,500
Developer's profit at 15% of sale price	52,000
Total development costs	280,000
Balance per site is 350,000 – 280,000 = 70,000	70,000
Assessed value of entire site = 50 units × 70,000 =	3,500,000

This sensitivity analysis gives a broad indication of potential values. While a detailed discounted cash flow analysis of all costs and revenues would provide a much better approximation of value, the volatility of development land markets is clearly illustrated by the major shifts in land prices resulting from house price shifts (see Table 3). An upward movement in house prices, with other inputs remaining fixed, has an exponential impact on land values which effectively double under an optimistic scenario, while a drop of 20 per

Table 3
Input sensitivity analysis – change scenarios – optimistic pessimistic

Input Change	+10% Unit Sale Price	+20% Unit Sale Price	-10% Unit Sale Price	-20% Unit Sale Price	Density Increase to 75 Units	Building Cost reduction of 10%	Building Cost reduction of 20%	Original Estimates
Residential Unit Sale Price	385,000	420,000	305,000	2,800,000	3,500,000	3,500,000	3,500,000	350,000
Total Develop-ment Cost	2,800,000	2,800,000	2,800,000	2,800,000	2,800,000	2,650,500	259,000	280,000
Balance per Site	105,000	140,000	25,000	0	70,000	84,500	91,000	70,000
Land Value	5,150,000	7,000,000	750,000	0	5,250,000	4,225,000	4,550,000	3,500,000
% Change in Land Value	47%	100%	-78%	-100%	50%	21%	30%	0%

cent in expected unit sale prices would result in a 100 per cent loss in land value and potential liquidation of the development company. Density increases are seen to significantly lift site values, while the benefit of locking down, or fixing costs at present levels where possible, is also clear.

With mixed-use developments and more complex commercial development schemes, a more detailed understanding of the nature of costs and revenues is needed. For local authorities and planning agencies, an understanding of a development appraisal allows an analysis of various development options and the resulting profits giving an economic basis for decision-making. In this worked example, a local authority owns a development site which they are advised is worth £10,000,000, which they can sell on the open market. Alternatively, the local authority or any owner may wish to retain some control by way of conditions in a joint venture agreement over future development, in addition to normal planning control and building legislation. This would be of importance to a public agency whose obligations would extend beyond maximising the commercial value of land assets. As an initial step, they could assess the development profitability of the site with the aim of sharing that gain with a development partner. The local authority may negotiate a sale at full market price or amend the asking price in return for community facilities/ affordable housing or other priorities, or seek to share in the development profits. All the estimates in the appraisal often included and analysed on a spreadsheet may be altered to give an estimate of different scenarios or outcomes. In turn, each of the inputs can be assessed individually to test the sensitivity of development profits to changes in costs or revenues.

In Table 4, the site which can accommodate a commercial development is assessed as having a potential development profit of over £14,000,000. This gives the participants, including the landowning partner, a clear idea of the possible negotiating positions they hold. In turn, both the landowner and potential partners will be examining the alternative scenarios based upon different development projects, costs and revenues. In turn, the spreadsheet can be used to test what effect individual input changes will have on appraisal outcomes independently – for example, a change in rentals achieved or combined where a rental or price increase occurs at the same time as a fall in interest rates and finance costs.

Frequently, potential gain is greatest where risk is also greatest, and the advantages of gains may compensate for the toleration of high levels of uncertainty. The calculations are based on the various participants' judgement and analysis of the regional property and development markets, future trends and the actions and decisions of other potential developers, investors and purchasers in the same market. A full analysis of all options on a proposed development will often involve a detailed exploration of a variety of options to establish potential profit, as outlined below.

Sensitivity analysis

All initial development valuations and appraisals must be based upon a considerable number of estimated inputs. The more

Table 4
Development appraisal to predict profit

Gross Development Value

Investment Value			
Rental Income		2,808,000.00	
Years Purchase based on Investment Yield	5.00%	20.00	
GDV		56,160,000.00	
Less Purchaser's Costs	5.75%	3,053,617	
NDV			53,106,383

Site Cost

Site			
Site Purchase Price		10,000,000.00	
Acquisition Costs	5.75%	575,000.00	
Total Site Cost			10,575,000.00

Development Cost

Construction Costs			
Area of Building	13,000 sq m		
Construction	£1,600 per sq m	20,800,000.00	
Contingency	10.00%	2,080,000.00	
Statutory Costs		400,000.00	
Demolition		150,000.00	
Total Construction Cost			23,430,000

Other Development Costs:	
Total Fees Cost	£2,860,000
Finance Cost	£1,685,918
Letting Cost	£491,960
TOTAL COSTS	39,042,878
PROFITS	14,063,504

Table 4 *continued*

Sensitivity Analysis of Original 25.1% Profit to Changes in Inputs

Construction Costs	Investment Yields				
25.10%	7.00%	7.25%	7.50%	7.75%	8.00%
1,000	22.20%	19.61%	17.03%	14.45%	11.86%
1,100	18.05%	15.32%	12.59%	9.85%	7.12%
1,200	13.90%	11.02%	8.14%	5.26%	2.38%
1,300	9.75%	6.72%	3.70%	0.67%	-2.36%
1,400	5.61%	2.43%	-0.75%	-3.93%	-7.10%
1,500	1.46%	-1.87%	-5.19%	-8.52%	-11.84%
1,600	-2.69%	-6.17%	-9.64%	-13.11%	-16.59%

Note: Changes in inputs such as running this model with a rent reduced by 10 per cent significantly reduces the overall profitability of the project to below £9,000,000 and indicates the volatility of market profitability in an uncertain market, highlighting the need to assess carefully the sensitivity of inputs to change.

complex the scheme, the more likely it is that inaccuracies will occur. This places a premium on experience and up-to-date local market knowledge. The reliability of the outputs and results is dependent on the quality of information and data used in the analysis. Indicated in the table are the effects of changes in inputs such as rents, yields, building costs and interest rates on profit. Constant reworking of calculations or sensitivity analysis to demonstrate the influence on land values of rental value or other input alterations is relatively easy to assess with the use of spreadsheet packages; estimates of the effects on profit of rising or falling rental values/sale prices can be determined almost instantaneously.

In the recent volatile market period, the demand for more explicitly analytical evidence for property development appraisals has become even more important. While the standard approach remains to estimate whether a proposal or intended scheme is likely to prove viable, based upon assumptions made, this is usually accompanied by feasibility studies, discounted cash flow analysis and scenario testing based upon ranges of probable costs and returns. In particular, public/private partnerships may involve the appraisal of complex development options with cash flows on completed schemes. In cases like these, project-tailored appraisals may be developed in a user-friendly manner and options in terms of sensitivity analysis, phasing and financing can be looked at in greater detail by all participants.

From this type of analysis it can be seen that changes to the various components of rent, yield, cost, finance and time can have dramatic effects upon the profitability of a scheme when tested as illustrated in Tables 3 and 4. This shows the sensitivity of key inputs in the initial appraisal to expected or unexpected changes. In Table 3 the volatility in the residential market is illustrated as movements downwards of 10 per cent in residential sale prices dramatically decrease the land value from £5 million pounds to less than £1 million pounds. This approach can also be adjusted to identify a breaking point at which a satisfactory level of profit can be obtained or a break-even point for the construction of affordable housing in each development situation.

Table 4 illustrates a commercial development situation where a profit of £14 million pounds is expected. If a second running of this appraisal is undertaken, with a rental reduction of 10 per cent inputted, this results in a decrease in profit from £14 million pounds to less than £9 million pounds. With a Discounted Cash Flow (DCF) approach, a developer, public agency or any partner in a development project can run multiple estimates of crucial inputs to determine the timing of costs and revenues, along with analysing risks and returns involved, as is shown in Table 5.

Following Table 4 we can see that sensitivity analysis can be used to examine the effect on the profit determined in the initial analysis of the combined potential changes in a number of key inputs, using the example of a range of investment yields and construction costs. It is clear that the impact on the expected development profit is significant if construction costs escalate significantly, as shown on the vertical axis, with losses being incurred as costs per metre squared go above £1,600, with changes in the expected market yield and impact on profit expected shown on the horizontal axis. This allows a spreadsheet statistical analysis of the outcomes in terms of profit across a range of scenarios and an assessment of what deviations might occur, along with the result of the most probable inputs and their outcomes. Advanced modelling or simulation can also include an input of probability weighting of each input and a simulation of various scenarios.

Discounted Cash Flow (DCF)

Discounted cash flow analysis is often used by developers as it is considered to produce a more accurate basis for analysis and appraisal of the development situation. The principal advantage of using cash flows is that there is considerably more flexibility in assessing the timing of all payments and receipts over the life of the project. As the same information (costs and values) is used initially in simplified residuals and cash flows, inaccuracies in any input will lead to errors, whichever method or approach is adopted. In negotiations with an investment and development appraisal focus, discounted cash flow approaches are regularly used. The standard net present value (NPV) approach involves the discounting of all inflows and outflows to establish their present value. The computation of the sum of discounted inflows and outflows produces the net present value of the development profit now. Individual developers have their own 'target' discount rates, but for initial appraisals it is logical to use a target rate above the short-term finance rate as this represents the real costs at that point in time. A positive NPV indicates that, allowing for the time cost of money, the scheme is profitable, and a negative NPV indicates on the same basis that a loss is likely. A discounted cash flow analysis can be carried out on all elements of any project. In the example below, a DCF analysis of a development project scenario is included. Table 5 illustrates an example of DCF being used to analyse the flow of construction costs across a project with its timing indicated. This would be important from both a cash flow and a borrowing perspective.

Table 5
Sample discounted cash flow

Month		0	1	2	3	4	5
Date		April 2019	May 2019	June 2019	July 2019	August 2019	
Site Cost		-6,000,000					
Aquisition Costs		-345,000					
Construction			-403,200	-672,000	-1,209,600	-1,612,800	
Preliminary Works			-10,000				
Fees			-175,720	-175,720	-175,720	-175,720	-175,720
Agent/ Letting							
NDV							
NCF		-6,345,000	-588,920	-847,720	-1,385,320	-1,788,520	-2,998,120
PV Factor	0.72%	1.0000	0.9928	0.9857	0.9787	0.9717	0.9647
PV Value		-6,345,000	-584,706	-835,631	-1,355,793	-1,737,874	-2,892,375

Knowing which factors are most sensitive to change and movement plays a critical role in decisions to initiate or defer development and provides a basis for the evaluation of partnership arrangements in the property development process. In carrying out detailed analyses, use is made of a conventional spreadsheet to give computer-aided calculations of numerous variations of the inputs involved. With this type of knowledge on the operations of the property development process, it is possible to examine the partnership arrangements in context and assess their ongoing impact on decision-makers in the process.

Key inputs in negotiations

With the benefit of this analysis it is possible to isolate those factors which are crucial to the decision-making process. Obviously with variables such as site development costs and professional fees, while their movement improves or reduces the relative feasibility of the project, their effect is not the most critical. Similarly, items such as agents' fees and advertising costs do not contribute a significant element of costs or revenues.

For large-scale commercial developments, small movements in land prices are also not significant, and savings in this area, while welcome, would not swing major development decisions. It is when rentals, investor yields, construction costs and finance costs are analysed that the greatest levels of uncertainty and risk are encountered.

Rental income is the developer's forecast of what rent will be achieved when the development is completed. This forecast is shaped by considerations of location and supply and demand in the market at a future point in time. Specialist advice from leading real estate experts or chartered surveyors will often be sought regarding expected levels at completion date. Normally, appraisals are based upon today's levels of rentals and cost. Expected rentals are difficult to predict as they are dependent on both supply and demand, with the intentions of other potential suppliers of development space unknown. Consequently, it is common practice to include in feasibility studies a series of rental levels. This assessment is crucial as it determines the expected capital value of the property from which the developer expects to derive the profits.

Investor yields are similarly crucial in their role in determining the expected capital value of the property developed. As a multiple of the rental in assessment of gross development value (GDV), the smallest change in yields significantly influences GDV and development profits. The sensitivity of these two factors combined produces the crucial estimate as to what revenues can be expected from a project.

Construction cost constitutes a major fixed cost on the development. If a variation is allowed in this factor due to inflation, wage increases, demand for building services or costs of raw materials, the effect is immediately to reduce development profits. Developers may attempt to contain construction costs through maximising competition by tender between potential building contractors. Cost savings are also often sought by delaying payment to the contractor, usually through phasing arrangements. During periods of low construction activity this process of cost reduction and competition is at its most intense, involving both initial tender price and phasing arrangements. Boom periods allow contractors to increase their tender prices and profits in the knowledge that competition is less pressing.

In 2019, the cost of finance is difficult to predict. The ready availability of low-cost finance from 2000 to 2007 contrasts with previous high costs based on historically high real interest rates in the 1980s and 1990s which made finance prohibitively expensive on many projects. Movement on finance cost is potentially more complex and more damaging than changes in other cost factors. Changes with major impact can occur either in time or interest rates which significantly affect profitability.

With such a high degree of sensitivity to change present in factors which are only reasoned assumptions, the scale of risk involved is often great. Variations of only 10 or 20 per cent in inputs – as indicated in Table 3 – can potentially either double or entirely remove profits. Great care and attention must therefore be taken in arriving at such estimates. While architects or quantity surveyors can, with a reasonable degree of confidence, predict building costs, the estimates of unit sale prices, rentals and yields must be regarded as less certain. The cost of finance, based as it is on time factors pertaining to the development as well as general economic considerations and government policy, is obviously out of the control and expertise of developers and property markets. Best estimates of the input figures included must therefore be based on probability analysis.

Timing of development remains the greatest imponderable since developments will only be coming onto uncertain markets at a future date. The final decision on development, phasing of development and timing of completion and final sale is therefore based on a series of crucial assessments and estimates. Based on analysis of these figures, any development interest, local authority or planning agency involved in development decisions can use appraisal tools to inform any decision-making processes. A rigorous appraisal process will aid the evaluation of what set of results is most probable, and finally, all participants need to establish if that crucial element of market timing is correct.

Appendix

Technical terms and abbreviations

For detailed descriptions, see 'RICS Valuation – Global Standards 2017 Incorporating the IVSC International Valuation Standards', issued June 2017, effective from 1 July 2017.

Development Appraisal
This is an appraisal of a potential development project to establish the total revenues and costs and surplus or residual value arising from development.

NPV – Net Present Value
Costs and revenues occur over a series of time periods. To evaluate the present value of all such costs and revenues at a single point in time, the concept of net present value is used to bring each of the revenue or cost items to their present value. The standard NPV formula used is NPV = F / [(1 + I) ^n] where F is the future cash flow, I is the interest rate and n is the number of years or time periods.

DCF – Discounted Cash Flow
This examines – using spreadsheet analysis – the series of revenues/costs occurring over the period of a project which are discounted to NPV to give a summation of all costs and revenues now or at the present time of the appraisal.

GDV – Gross Development Value
The total value or revenue expected from the completed development.

DC – Development Costs
The total of all direct and indirect costs of achieving the development.

Gross Construction Area
The total area constructed, including areas in common and letting areas.

Net Letting Area
The area of the proposed development which can be let and can gain revenue. In a commercial development this will typically be over 10 per cent lower than the gross area constructed.

Scenario Sensitivity Analysis
The results of development appraisals or residual values are the result of subtracting total costs from revenues. A small percentage change in either number has the potential to make a large percentage change in the resulting final amount. Due to this sensitivity, multiple changes in the critical variables in the model are often tested.

Chapter 4 Property Development and Financing Development

Property development

Planning and policy decisions will often involve negotiations with market interests; therefore, an understanding of property market operations and financing requirements is essential. For commercial development projects a working knowledge of both market trends and market decision processes is a fundamental starting point to informed negotiations. The market for urban space is related to economic markets of other types in that supply/demand relationships are expressed through property price mechanisms that regulate levels of activity. This chapter outlines why the concept of the perfect market, as formulated in basic economic doctrine developed by Adam Smith and others since the eighteenth century, is not always appropriate for the property market. This occurs as the imperfections and uncertainties of the real property market and the complexity of the multiple variables which tend to influence its movement take analysis of the market beyond conventional economic theory. It is necessary to recognise that investment in property, whether for utility or market return, is but one part of the overall investment market and that there are numerous factors which make this form of investment unique and often subject to both high risk and high return.

Planning, public policy and governance issues play an important role in urban development, both in the provision of appropriate urban space, infrastructure and services for economic and business functions and in public policy in all fields of urban infrastructure and restructuring. Direct provision of public services and development is clearly dependent on the state of public finances and economic planning and development processes. Public financial support for other development activities can range from indirect tax incentives to direct public shareholding in development projects. Historically, the state in many European countries has been instrumental in economic development activities. The state has been the main provider of infrastructure upon which all development and economic activity depends. Public regional or city banks in many areas of Germany provide an important and active role in city development activities. In other European countries, including the UK and Ireland, many regional development agencies have provided capital, buildings and other support to new enterprises. It is evident that both the level and type of state intervention differs widely internationally. This is particularly evident in examining the differing state responses to managing urban development processes in the public interest.

A traditional view of property development had a focus on national banking systems, with decisions based on regional demand and supply responses. This approach prioritised the role of development and investment finance, with changing interest rates and capital availability viewed at a national or regional level as a driver of property cycles. Lower interest rates were seen to boost the property market while higher interest rates were understood to dampen property demand and development activity. In recent decades, we have seen a significant change, with a trend to increased globalisation in property investment and finance whereby international providers of capital increasingly play a critical role.

This trend can be represented as changing the role of urban property and infrastructure development from a regional planning and development supply response to a vehicle for capital switching at a global scale, with an over-accumulation of international capital seeking out investment destinations at a global scale to maximise returns. The property market has moved swiftly from the previous local/regional model, which largely involved a relatively small group of regional/national development interests funded by local financial banking, and institutional interests with a regular working arrangement liaising with local planning officials.

Development activity in urban areas is now largely dependent on inputs of private sector investment capital as public funding for such schemes has been reducing. This trend is accelerated by the increasing role allocated to public/private partnerships in a broad range of development areas previously dealt with by the public sector, including health and education infrastructure.

The relationship between construction activity, the general economy, property investment, development and decision-making provides the essential background against which new directions in planning and policy initiatives can be assessed. Policies which improve the functioning of these various activities and their participants can form an important part of proactive development approaches. Equally, policies which make an already complicated process more complex may be inefficient, inequitable or both. Improving the nature of supply and demand for the various sectors of the property market and the interplay between investors, developers, financiers, consumers and policy-makers would seem fundamental to success if the processes of planning and development are to benefit all participants.

The property market and the supply of urban built space

The general economy is the prime generator of demand for increased development and construction activity (Wyatt, 2007).[1] Such activity is directly linked to the performance of the real economy, and periods of buoyant output and growth generally coincide with periods of high economic growth in the regional and national economy. The logic of this correlation is that increases in disposable incomes lead to increased demand and retail sales, leading to increases in demand for retail space. Similarly, growth in employment leads to increased demand for housing, industrial and office space (Dubben and Williams, 2009).[2]

The overall increase in economic wealth results in increased investment in social and economic infrastructure. Planned

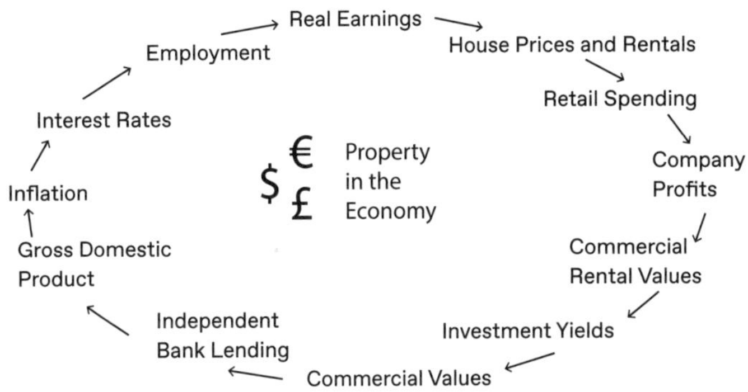

Figure 10
Property in the economy

improvements and additions to the urban environment are generated by and paid for by general economic activity and resulting public revenues and resources (O'Sullivan, 2019).[3] The resultant demands for built space can both increase exchequer tax flows and provide funds for such development. Figure 10 outlines key linkages between property markets and the real economy. Reduced demand can, in turn, lead to decline, vacancy, blight and dereliction.

The greater volatility in construction activity over GDP that is often experienced, represents the effects of factors other than economic performance influencing the system. Related factors, such as population movement, sector-specific issues and the impact of taxation incentives and disincentives, can result in significant changes in patterns of construction activity. Additionally, while the funding of a major part of all property development is private, the significance of public sector investment in both infrastructure and public building programmes is of major importance. Often the linkages are considerably weaker or counter-cyclical as the state may attempt to fund and initiate such activities in times of economic downturn, and indeed, often during such times, will attempt to maintain or increase its activity to maintain or stimulate growth.

Within the commercial development sector, the linkage with economic activity is most evident within the speculative element of the market. Anticipating changes in demand or supply, where sector demand appears under-supplied, involves an awareness of movements in the real economy along with the resultant sector movements in the property markets. Structural changes within the economy similarly may result in significant changes in sector demand, which will result in increased development activity. For public sector development projects, the decision-making process for development is heavily influenced by socio-economic factors. The nature of decision-making processes by the public sector can entail the prioritisation of certain projects or sectors based upon cost/benefit analysis and conditioned by the administrative and political context in which such decisions are taken.

Demand and activity generated by owner-occupiers is not as strongly linked to GDP movement, since their land use, maintenance and improvement decisions are largely dictated and fixed by their present land use at their existing locations. Investment and speculative new development, in contrast, can be seen to significantly expand as a region's economy grows and contracts as expectations of slower growth become established. However, as land prices and construction costs may tend to be lower during a recessionary period or trough in the pattern of development activity, owner-occupiers tend to develop and maintain a reasonable rate of construction output during these periods. As the bulk of commercial development is carried out and financed by private development interests within the UK markets, the pattern of boom and bust has tended to dominate the commercial sectors.

The contributory elements of property development, investment and real demand tend to result in surges of development and oversupply causing effectively the next correction or depression in the property market. This is caused by imperfections within the market processes producing the built environment, with the role of public sector development activities often tending to parallel private development activity rather as that might be expected, acting as a stabilising influence on the process.

With the public sector financing a large share of total output in the construction industry, it is perhaps surprising that the state does not instead adopt a role of counter-cyclical stabilisation of the industry. Funding and assisting development activity during economic downturns, it can be argued, would prevent markets overheating, remove instability in labour markets and result in a more even development pattern. Evidence over time and regions would suggest, however, that this pattern tends to be repeated internationally (Barras, 1994).[4]

Building cycles, associated with periodic large expansions in investment in property development, have been acknowledged as a feature of many economies and linked with international movements of population and capital, as well as with other economic features such as interest rates, commodity and resource prices.

Demand for construction activity and completed development space is therefore the key element in understanding this cyclical process of development and construction activity. This demand arises from two potential pools, the user market for such property that will either own or rent, and the property investment market. These two markets evolve from the ability to separate ownership and the occupation rights, allowing separate interests to develop in the same property. Real estate occupiers, particularly from the commercial sector operating in central areas, frequently find the capital costs of purchasing a property high relative to current income. Acquisition may therefore involve commitment of substantial capital resources which could be more profitably invested in the occupier's core business activity. Costs of interest on capital borrowed, management and maintenance costs and the management resources needed to acquire and maintain a property will often be regarded as being substantially higher than the rental costs now or in the future.

This results in a market for commercial property such as offices and retail on a rented basis. The property investment market exists to supply property at an adequate return to this occupier market. The basis for adequate returns on property investments is generally regarded as stability of income in real terms and rising capital values (Baum and Crosby, 2007).[5] These two separate markets for property – occupier demand and investment deman – are most obviously prevalent in central areas of major cities where the agglomeration of business users results in high capital values, making the ownership of property sufficiently attractive for major investment interests. Its operation is particularly noted in the office development market in major growth centres such as London or Paris, where the relative scale of capital values and investment required is highest.

While investment in property, whether for utility or market return, is but one part of the overall investment market, there are numerous factors which make this form of investment unique. Investment in general terms can be defined as the giving up of the present use of capital for potential future income return or capital gain. This return can be by way of rent for investors or by way of rent foregone and occupational benefits for occupiers. In central city areas, long-term investment capital seeks to purchase properties for leasing purposes to receive long-term flows of income. In doing so, such interests may develop a dominant role in the market.

Differences between property and other commodities available for investment purposes begin with the heterogeneous nature of each individual property investment. Unique factors such as its location, design, function and other characteristics have positive and negative investment consequences. Positively, this uniqueness can contribute to fixity in supply in that, in general terms, the purchaser of a prime location investment property at a key location in a central city expects a high level of continuing demand for this property. As most buildings have a long life and additions to stock are relatively small, demand tends to focus on existing stock and especially at traditional prime/high value or key locations. The standard investment has a freehold commercial building let at its full rental value with a lease guaranteeing rental income regularly reviewed upwards in line with market trends over decades.

The security of this investment is often assisted by the inelasticity of supply as the number of suitable sites is relatively fixed, mainly already pre-empted by existing alternative users. Difficulties involving site assembly in older historic central areas, legislative restrictions and the planning and bye-law processes can involve lengthy delays in any alternative developments of premises coming to the market. Because the rental income is a prior charge on a company or tenant, irrespective of profits or loss, and because of the fact that the property can be re-let should that tenant's business fail, this can enhance the security of income to the investor.

Other advantages of property as an investment are the ability to select the size of investments to suit the varying capital requirements of investors, and the availability of preferential tax arrangements and incentives associated with property investment in specified sectors or areas. The selection and management of property investments to achieve many or all the benefits discussed requires identification of current and future market trends and can involve rigorous standards of selection. The many disadvantages associated with incorrect investment decisions lead some potential investors to concentrate their development activity on prime areas or sectors only. This results in significant pressure for investment and development in existing prime areas which involve the historic core of the city, and neglect of other secondary areas which, despite being ready for and needing development and investment activity, present higher risks than established prime locations. In terms of partnership negotiations, it is those areas in need of major investment and development which are often in focus. The need to attract investment to areas in need of renewal is often a reason for interventions or the public sector seeking to attract private partners to invest in such areas. Figure 11 shows the relevant relationships and processes.

The chief disadvantages attached to investment in property arise with the large initial sums needed to enter the market. Prices for the smallest commercial investment property available, for example, in the London market would frequently be more than £10,000,000, while the larger investments can involve sums over £100,000,000. Entry to such markets is beyond the capability of

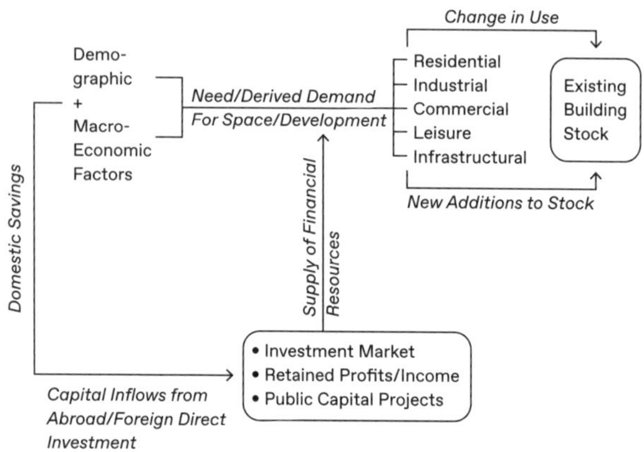

Figure 11
Relationships and processes in property development

many private investors and the market was in the past dominated by the larger financial institutions such as pension funds and life assurance companies. Smaller investors have tended to focus on residential markets and the buy-to-let sector.

The financial institutions benefit from large-scale, long-term contractual inflows of funds, with outflows from present income not required in the medium term. Their availability of capital ensures that other potential purchasers are often at a disadvantage in competing with such institutions. The special tax treatment of the return on investments (for example, rent enjoyed by the financial institutions such as pension funds) similarly gives a competitive advantage in the marketplace. Financial institutions, including pension funds, have a fiduciary duty or responsibility to match their assets and future liabilities. For example, their 2019/20 intake of new pension contribution streams or life assurance policies might be expected to be invested to meet their need for matching payments as such policies mature in 2059/60, or the date specified in such policies.

The frequently high costs of transfer and liquidity problems with property assets make such investment difficult for many individual investors who might require the capital for alternative uses in the short term. Legal, professional and acquisition taxes make entry into the market prohibitive and, while costs of transfers inhibit certain investors, it is the potential losses in forced sale situations which may deter many, but not the longer-term investor. While a pension fund or life assurance company may be able to hold property through a downturn or series of downturns in the property cycle, it is unlikely that many private investors would have enough resources to do so. Again, the institutional long-term investor can take such risks and look at the timescales required for such investment positions, to the exclusion of other market participants.

Subjective valuation monitoring and evaluation makes the actual performance of major property investment particularly difficult to monitor over time. The open market value of a property is clear in its true sense only on its purchase date and final date of sale. However, all estimates of value during the intervening period are subjective and may be proved incorrect if put to the market for sale or disposal. Issues such as the responsibility for management, maintenance and continual improvements and repairs required on all buildings also make investment in property challenging for the non-specialist investor in property.

The biggest risk that any investor in property faces is the obvious impact of changes in demand, creating falling returns. Changes in demand resulting in downward pressure in rental prices and capital prices can occur due to structural changes in the economy affecting sector demand, real economic decline, obsolescence of the individual building or an oversupply occurring. While a decline in the national or local economy cannot be discounted in the decision-making process other than by deferral of investment, rational choices can be made which minimise risk if investment is decided upon. Changes in demand and obsolescence of building type or function are less likely to affect prime property, often described as modern commercial property at good locations suitable and adaptable for modern needs and for alternative users if required. Risk minimisation, therefore, leads many investors in property internationally to focus their efforts on this sector. The combination of resource availability, taxation considerations, and complex management expertise requirements and the key knowledge and experience of the workings of an imperfect market therefore give large-scale investors a pivotal role in the shape of major development projects.

The returns sought from investment in property are normally expressed as a yield, which is the periodic return from an investment expressed as a percentage of the capital sum invested. In turn, capital values are expressed as a multiple of rental income, the multiple being derived from the level of initial yield or return required. Higher perceptions of risk lead to requirements for high initial yields, while lower yields or return are acceptable on investments which represent low risk of losses and upon which growth in rental and capital income is expected. This inter-relationship between the two sectors of the demand present in the property market is of vital importance. Good investments which produce a good return require strong tenant demand, and in turn, the supply of adequate space for tenants is dependent on adequate returns being available for investors.

Market prices at which investment properties are sold can normally be assessed by the following relationship: capital value = rental multiplied by 100 divided by the level of initial yield or return required. If the initial yield required is 5 per cent and the rental is £100,000, this will give a resulting capital value of £100,000 multiplied by 100 over 5, which is 100,000 multiplied by 20, giving a capital value of £2,000,000.

Initial yields at which prime office property is purchased in the current markets can range from 3 to 5 per cent. This obviously greatly exceeds returns currently available, with interest on deposits in banks in the recent period as low as 1 to 3 per cent. Even in periods of higher bank interest rates exceeding 3 per cent, property has attracted high levels of investment due to the primary importance of the continuation of rental growth as, if included in calculations, initial yields of 3 or 5 per cent will often achieve target rates of return of 8–10 per cent on investments. This focus on a search for rental growth provided one of the great attractions of property investment, particularly during inflationary periods such as the 1990s. A desire to outpace the general rate of inflationary growth has in the past attracted investment funds to property. If the trend in the twenty-first century towards lower inflation levels continues, this 'hedge against inflation' attribute of property assets becomes less important. Indeed, the high costs of refurbishment of property and the need to make allowances for depreciation and obsolescence of all property tend to become more recognised during periodic downturns in the property market when strong rental growth is no longer guaranteed.

During weaker market periods the concentration of investors is often on improving the return from existing investment by increasing the rental return where possible. This can be achieved by either the refurbishment of buildings to upgrade their function to a higher paying level within their existing use, or to a higher value use, for example, residential to office. The supply of built space is dependent on the successful matching of supply, demand and development finance and expertise, as indicated in Figure 12.

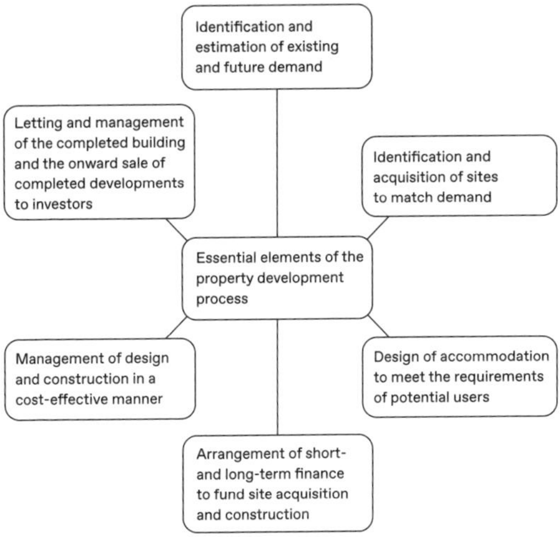

Figure 12
Essential elements of property development

Finance and the development process

Availability of finance can play a vital role in two of the key stages in property development: initial project finance and investment finance. First, the short-term costs of the developer in borrowing the necessary capital to initiate and then complete the process are crucial for the development of property to occur. Following completion of the development, the onward sale of that project and its retention as an investment by an owner-occupier or investor involves the availability of capital for such transfers over a longer term.

Short-term project finance is necessary for the purchase of the site, payment of professional and other fees, payments to contractors for construction work, etc. In the case of a property development company, finance is often sought on an interest-only payment arrangement or scheme, with final repayment on a roll-up basis at completion and sale of the project. At this stage, the project capital, plus any remaining compounded interest, is repaid in a lump sum. Larger property development companies could fund developments from their own resources of retained earnings or by a stock market issue to raise capital. However, most developments would be carried out with at least part borrowed capital.

While the main clearing banks would often provide short-term working capital, it is the specialist business or merchant banks which have, historically, dominated such business. Short-term working capital from clearing banks would often only be available at levels which were above variable interest rates and subject to short-term recall. Loans from merchant banks or finance houses were alternatively negotiated at fixed rates for a term of years. Such loans would be the preferred source for property company finance intended for speculative development activity. Availability of such finance significantly affects the supply of development, as without this input development does not occur. Banking groups as lenders are clearly taking a risk in lending on speculative developments and some arrangements reflect a further extension of this risk with equity-sharing arrangements. In these arrangements the lender takes a stake or equity in the proposed development as part of the funding arrangement.

The risks involved in development financing were starkly illustrated in the last decade when poorly regulated financial and property markets were a clear contributory factor in the global Great Financial Crisis, and planning and policy interests will be expected to use their powers to prevent an occurrence of a similar crisis in the future. Financial decision-making clearly became disconnected from analysis of risk and returns. Expansions of lending were not based on repayment capacities but often on the desire to expand the loan base and resulting bonuses. Real risk was effectively eventually borne by the state with the socialisation of losses associated with property lending in many countries including Ireland, the UK, the US and Germany. After banking failures and state rescues of the financial system it seems likely that in the future the main banks will have a reduced role in the property market, with the current cycle more dependent on equity financing than debt.

In 2019, institutional investors are still a feature of regional markets seeking stable income from a secure and hopefully appreciating asset. The significant reductions in bond yields have diverted many national and international institutional investors and large wealth management funds towards property investment. This internationalisation or financialisation of the urban development process is seen in turn as creating a risk of more pronounced short-term cyclical patterns as such investment capital is constantly mobile and seeking new markets to optimise returns.

There is also a risk of creating asset bubbles, including in the real estate sector as local and international investors all focus on prime property sectors in regions already experiencing high growth. These groups include both long-term investors such as pension funds and hedge or private equity funds whose actions in the property market may often be short-term – acquiring property cheaply in distressed markets to sell or flip the assets quickly as the market turns.

Traditional property companies, both public and private, retain an important role. This group, while including the traditional regional/national developers and property companies, has been augmented by real estate investment trusts (REITs) with a focus on securing long-term income. The aim of an REIT is to add value to the assets they acquire and own, and to pay regular dividends to their investors. Investors investing in property as a store for wealth include high-net-worth individuals or sovereign wealth funds with long-term asset management strategies. Equity investors act as lenders who take a fixed stake in a property development. In many ways the criteria they use to decide on project funding logically follow similar criteria to those which should be used by any prudent lender. In contrast with asset management funds – which are sometimes termed 'vulture funds', as they actively pursue acquisitions in distressed markets at discounted prices – REITs were often promoted as having a long-term commitment to the region in which they operate. REITs can borrow from banks and as they evolve, they become more like the regional property companies from which some of such entities evolved. While the stabilisation and recovery of bank lending operations is ongoing, the role of banking activities related to property development lending is now moving back to the traditional prudential criteria upon which such loans were granted, and often have regard to the following factors in Figure 13.

In a weak market, the forward sale or letting of any proposed development is often viewed as essential. This effectively pushes the development market to a situation where development is only viable where future occupation is guaranteed or where the developer can utilise funds generated internally. Additionally, in the present situation, lending institutions have recognised and reduced their exposure to what is now seen as a higher risk sector. Such portfolio considerations and management of risk apply both to lending institutions and borrowers. International experience is that over-exposure to the speculative property sector leads to major problems in the banking system such as has periodically occurred in the early 1970s, 1990s and again in the 2007/8 Great Financial Crisis.

The standard mortgage-type loan has diminished in importance as few developers would commit themselves to speculative ventures on this basis, even if such loans were still

Real Estate Investment Trusts (REITs)

In recent years asset management companies and funds representing the wealth of sovereign states have engaged in property investment and development, and Real Estate Investment Trusts or Funds (REITs) have become active participants in development markets. REITs also enable individual smaller investors to access the general property investment market. Such investors in property acting individually and purchasing buy-to-let properties for investment can end up taking on property management and landlord functions. Instead, through investing in REITs, they effectively pool resources and responsibilities. This gives investors the critical mass necessary to invest in larger scale commercial properties and apartment blocks rather than individual units. REITs in turn often have property management arms which undertake the professional management of all aspects of property management.

REITs are tax-transparent property investment vehicles for investors. Many REITs are property companies which have converted to REITs. All the profits are passed to shareholders and the REIT acts in the same manner as a property investment company except in relation to reduced tax liabilities. In effect two stages of taxation are liable on investors in property company shares, with corporation tax paid by the company and shareholders paying income tax. An REIT, in contrast, directly pays at least 90 per cent of rental income as dividends which are subject to personal taxation at lower rates than income taxes, with UK dividend taxation levels starting with a basic rate of 7.5 per cent in 2018/2019.

REITs were especially active in the recovering property markets in the Eurozone area in the past decade. Governments hoped that the entry of REITs would significantly aid recovering property markets and boost the supply process with new developments. To date REITs have proved to be significant investors in such markets without yet boosting supplies. They have become a major player in the purchase of completed new developments and can effectively outbid other purchasers of affordable housing – such as first-time buyers – with their critical mass and professional resources. These groups were especially active during the trough of the recession, with a capability to purchase distressed assets at discounted prices.

With recovery in such markets the opportunities for discounted purchases will lessen and sales onward are occurring as both REITs and wealth management act to achieve best returns for their stakeholders. They do not have a responsibility to provide for the needs of local and regional markets and in fact can be highly mobile and constantly searching for the best next opportunities to purchase assets on the international markets in regions where, for whatever reason, such assets are undervalued and local market participants lack the capital to avail of such opportunities.

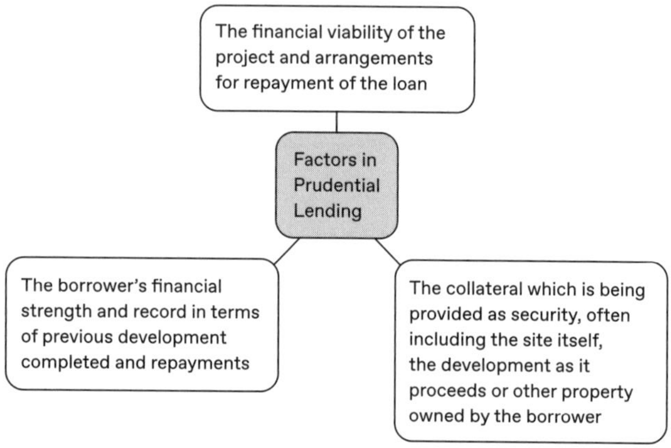

Figure 13
Key factors of prudential lending

available. The continual strong rental growth of the 1960s saw enough revenue returns guaranteed to cover mortgage capital and interest repayments which were often based on fixed interest rates. Increasing inflation rates meant that repayments were increasingly unattractive in terms of return for the lending institutions which increasingly sought a greater share of the returns being generated by the development process.

Instead of developers building and selling on, often with large capital gains, investing institutions sought and obtained equity participation in major projects which they were financing. Arrangements for such partnership or equity-sharing arrangements are numerous and often involve ground rent-type agreements including combinations of landowners, developers, contractors and financial institutions. The share of profits from resulting rental income is normally based on the inputs of the various parties and can be shared in a variety of models, as discussed in Figure 8.

The trend since the 1990s has been for elements of the financing of development projects to merge with the investment process. This switch from debt to equity financing accelerated in the aftermath of the Great Financial Crisis.

Major risks undertaken in financing speculative development entail a major risk of losses in the event of the project's failing. Owners of capital reserves and lending institutions therefore extended their role to overlap with that of investors, with common forms of long-term financing emerging which combine both roles. A large range of financing models has evolved including forward sales and sale and leaseback as indicated in the box below.

Financing models

Forward sale: A typical developer is involved in short-term trading in property rather than long-term investment. As finance is difficult to obtain, a prior agreement with an investor who will purchase or 'take out' a completed development is desirable in an uncertain market. Such agreements include precise details of the sale arrangements, including effects of delays, voids in letting, expected rental pattern, etc., between the funder and the developer. As the investor's main concern is the full rental value on completion, while the developer balances the potential profit derived from such rental with the risk of uncertain demand on completion, negotiations involve a trade-off between potential profit and risk.

Sale and leaseback: This evolved as a popular term of long-term financing which involves a developer selling the freehold interest in a completed development to an investor and taking back a long lease on the property at a rent equal to the initial yield as reflected in the selling price. The developer then takes on the management of the completed project and aims to sublet the property at a rent above that paid to the investor.

Mezzanine finance: Major development projects can require borrowing from several sources. Often a conventional bank borrowing arrangement will only provide 60 per cent to 80 per cent of the amount required, necessitating a 'final slice' or 'top up' arrangement. This 'top up' can sometimes come from a series of banks or a syndicate and will often be at a higher risk rate than the main loan as the developer's main assets may already have been used as collateral to secure the main loan. Often regarded as high risk, these loans will be at high interest rates or involve shares of the eventual profits. Such finance is often regarded as outside conventional banking arrangements, highly speculative and possibly dubious as regards the business ethics of consultants who are often involved in setting up deals. Statutory authorities internationally have expressed concerns as to the source and eventual ownership of large-scale funds often moving through property assets. The role of off-shore funds in property investment where final ownership is unclear is a concern in many jurisdictions.

The general deregulation of investment and financial markets since the 1990s led to considerable inflows of funds into property development. Free movement of capital, combined with complex specialised financial arrangements, created major flows of funds available internationally for property development and investment. This climate of ever-increasing property values and strong investment-led development growth created large levels of confidence in property markets throughout Europe into the twenty-first century. Finance was widely available, and the market seemed to be on a continual upward trend. It was in this climate that significant levels of international private finance were willing to enter the property market. In the UK and elsewhere, investment in publicly quoted property development companies or unit trusts evolved which financed the many major developments of the period. Local and regional sources of funding were complemented by significant global flows of investment funding in all major property markets. Statutory agencies in the UK and Ireland attempted to channel these flows of finance to involve its participation in desired policy focus areas including in urban regeneration and Private Finance Initiatives.

Finally, at a national level, many jurisdictions also have tax-based property investment incentive programmes to stimulate and subsidise development activity. Such programmes are often linked to planning objectives for the regeneration of secondary locations. This form of finance, tax-driven and subsidised, was available for development activity in areas which were treated with caution by traditional sources of finance. Therefore, the lending preferences of traditional lenders to the property market were to some extent bypassed in the finance for development within special incentive designated areas such as enterprise zones. Such finance as would be provided for projects in secondary areas would normally involve the developer providing a large part of the equity himself/herself, requiring ownership of the land and the provision of both collateral and personal warranties.

In planning and public policy terms, debates persist about the evaluation of such schemes, balancing the success in attracting physical development financed or subsidised by taxation breaks with issues including: deadweight – meaning levels of projects which would have proceeded anyway and the levels of subsidy, whether optimum or excessive; market distortions caused by development and investment prioritisation, including the economic and social impact on existing communities; displacement and relocation of commercial users, including the shadow effect of new developments on old.

Chapter 5 Planning and Cyclical Property Market Processes, the Role of Market Prices and Property Market Analysis

Property prices and price cycles in a market economy

It may appear that prices are beyond the influence of planners, but planning can assist in supporting affordable supplies of housing and other sectors of the built environment to lessen market volatility, development shortages, surges and corrections. A firm understanding of the cyclical nature of market pricing and valuation systems which gives rise to movements, surges and corrections in pricing patterns is required.

Prices, as represented in rentals and capital sale prices, are the prime determinants of construction activity and the provision of new development. However, as much of urban space has been built for a considerable period, particularly in the centre of older urban areas, the factors which determine its use, refurbishment, redevelopment and obsolescence require examination.

The nature of the property market in its heavy dependence on large capital investments has significant implications for public economic policy. High interest rates can cause a shortage of development capital and supply of new property. Conversely low interest rates have been identified as a contributory factor in the oversupply of specific property categories and the encouragement of high land values. The volatility of the property development market can often be traced back to public policy or money supply. The cyclical nature of the property market identified in mixed economies introduces a high degree of risk and uncertainty into urban development markets.

Planning is significantly influenced by the prevalence of cycles as the nature of a development plan-led approach is that it is based on the market conditions at the creation of the plan. Fluctuations in markets have become more regular, creating uncertainty as to medium- and longer-term market issues.

Booms and slumps may not be beneficial to end-users in the long term as an inefficient development market may result, providing space at a higher price than an efficient or more stable market. Many construction and development interests involved in the speculative development process also do not benefit from the large degree of risk and uncertainty involved. Some will make large profits while others will lose heavily, depending on the timing of their investment decisions. Competition at all levels plays a major role in the culture of the property development industry.

The primary relationship between price and supply is illustrated in Figure 14. The relationship is represented by increasing prices or rentals on the vertical axis, with increasing quantities of residential units or commercial space provided across the horizontal axis. The impact of increases in market demand with resulting price increases acts as a major signal or stimulus to suppliers of space to increase supply levels from A1 to A2.

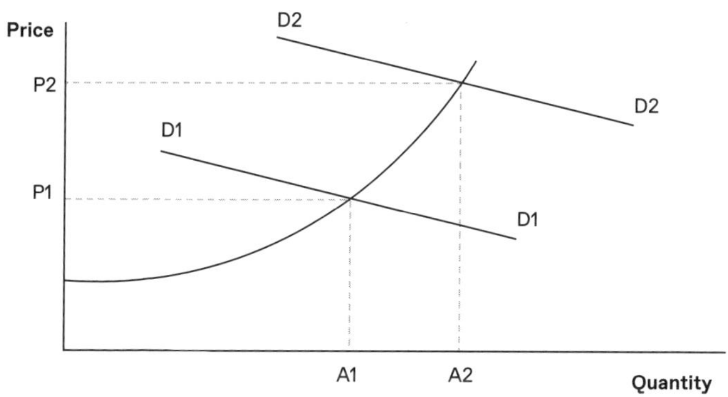

Figure 14
Property prices and supply/demand relationship

The process begins with quantity of accommodation fixed at A1, demand is indicated by demand line D1 which, through the interaction of supply and demand, has fixed the price of this type of space at P1. Improvement in the general economy leads to an increased level of demand D2 which, in competing for existing supplies, pushes the price level up to P2. At this new price, further accommodation is made available (A2). As the level of accommodation is relatively fixed in the short term, sudden changes in demand can lead to rapid price increases. Within a speculative development market, profit-seeking suppliers should respond to the new price level by increasing levels of accommodation.

The next issue for examination is that of time periods over which the property market operates and its impact on development patterns. Because of the different timeframes within which such changes in demand and output occur, development cycles and booms and slumps result (Williams and Reynolds-Feighan, 2015).[1] Demand for property can change very quickly due to improved economic activity, lower interest rates and increased confidence. However, the supply of built space often lags such increases in demand and in later stages of the cycle fails to respond to the levelling off or reduction of demand, as illustrated in Figure 15.

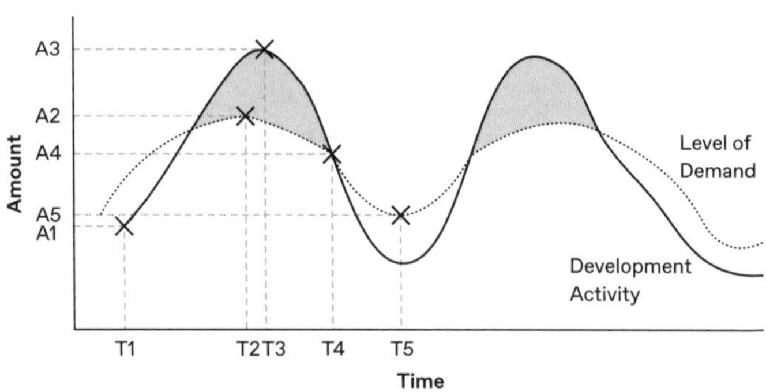

Figure 15
Cyclical interaction of demand and supply patterns

This example begins during a weak market phase during which development interests have been largely inactive and the economy and property market have been experiencing low growth. With weaker economic and market conditions, levels of development are run-down and the risk in market prospects leads to the cancellation or postponement of development decisions.

As a recovery or upswing eventually occurs at T1, the amount of development activity A1 lags demand, as the time for completion of projects will be a minimum of one to two years from initiation through planning to development. The impact of this time lag – with demand levels rising, even modestly – is to drive up rentals and lower yields on the available stock, making development activity substantially more profitable. As evidence of an increase in demand is analysed by development site owners, the expectations of profitability increase, as does the supply of new development. At this point in the market, financiers also become more willing to lend and the supply of property therefore rises to A3. With lead developments attracting sales and lettings at good profit levels, this encourages an increasing number of other developers to enter the marketplace. All are acting with imperfect market knowledge as to what the precise level of existing and future demand is.

Early entrants will have made high profits due to their having acquired sites for low prices during the weak phase of the market. However, later entrants will push up both land prices and levels of supply; this increase in supply reaching completion at T3 may already have created supply beyond available demand at T2. Nevertheless, the nature of development activity is that, once initiated, a construction project cannot be abandoned without incurring substantial losses. The timespan over which a project will take to move from inception to completion, two years or more, makes judgements of supply/demand relationships difficult, and occurrences of oversupply are common.

The result of oversupply is falling rentals and reduced investor demand, leading to decreased profitability. At this stage (T4) new development proposals have been suspended and major reductions in development activity occur. With little or no development occurring effectively, a correction or even over-correction in market activity levels results. Thus, the level of demand once it stabilises, even at low level, will tend after time to find supplies limited, leading to increasing rentals, the commencement of the next cycle and the tendency to repeat again the stages as already described at T5. The difficulty in recovering from a severe correction is evidenced in the Eurozone economies and the Irish housing market. The strong cyclical movement in the housing market illustrated below shows a boom period, peaking with an annual level of housing construction of 93,000 units, with supply collapsing to fewer than 10,000 units per annum in the following decade. Such volatility produced a crash in the property markets, with prices falling by up to 50 per cent (Williams and Nedović-Budić, 2016),[2] as illustrated in Figure 16. Ten years after the crash, property prices are now moving back to their previous levels; however, the supply process is still in recovery, with construction capacity issues and financing concerns evident still.

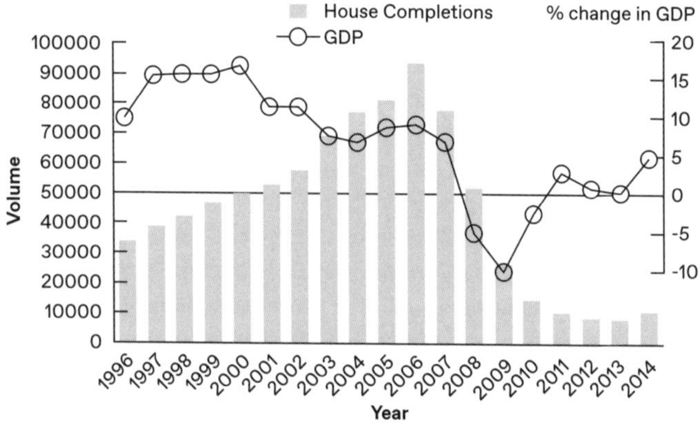

Figure 16
Property boom to crash – housing market, Ireland

Table 6
Typical property life cycle

Timescale Year	Phase/User	Condition	Costs	Revenue and Investment Return
-2	Feasibility and Site Purchase	–	–	Potentially High
-1	Design Proposals and Planning	–	–	Potentially High
0	Construction or Completion	New	Nil	High
1	New Business or Industry Single Users	New	Nil	High
10+	Established User	Good	Maintenance and Modification	Moderate
20+	Old Single User	Fair	Substantial Maintenance and Repair	Poor
25+	Mixture of Older and Emerging Users	Poor	Substantial Refurbishment Required	High
Option (A) 30+	Refurbishment/ Development	New	Nil	
Option (B) 30+	Vacant Obsolete	Derelict	Major	Nil/Vacant Site Tax

Life cycles in buildings, property prices and development implications

The economic cycle which dictates the utilisation and investment in buildings represents a pattern of replacement or refurbishment which occurs when the value of the site exceeds the existing building's real value, as indicated in Table 6. This increase in site value occurs due to the nature of the pricing system which reflects hope, or potential, values in site prices. As the real return declines, continuing growth in an urban area and the potential for new uses or more intensive uses inflate site values over time. Planning regulations, by way of conservation and preservation objectives, can act to delay or prevent the demolition of such buildings. However, refurbishment and intensification of use or changes of use should occur at the point at which the site value exceeds the existing property value.

Nevertheless, buildings in central city areas can be of such poor quality that refurbishment or redevelopment is not an economic option. This may occur due to the condition of existing buildings on difficult sites which are unsuitable for development because of site assembly problems, or legal difficulties. In such cases, the decay and neglect of property frequently leads to a deteriorating environment.

While cycles of demand in development activity dictate the overall level of development in urban areas, the existence of large areas of dereliction, pockets of vacant land and rundown buildings occur and remain even through cyclical upswings. Explanations for these seemingly contradictory pockets which defy general trends can be found by examination of the economics of development and redevelopment on an individual site basis. Lack of development at these locations and undesirable pressures for development in established areas often involves the aspirations of the planning process being directly opposite to the intentions of the speculative development interests. The basis for this conflict is the development interest's desire to maximise profit. This will often not consider externalities or the costs and effects of new development on the public and other land users, and differ from planners' wishes to achieve the objectives of their development plan without their own resources to achieve implementation. The reality of this situation is that development profit is the area in which the essential trade-off between the private market's wishes and the planners' objectives occurs (Williams and Reynolds-Feighan, 2015).[3] This process of obsolescence and redevelopment is illustrated in Figure 17.

In Figure 17, the relationship between site prices, building prices and real demand is demonstrated. The relative relationship between prices and time dictates critical points at which development decisions are made. At Price 1 (P1) the initial relationship at inception of site value, situated at one third of building value, has moved to parity.

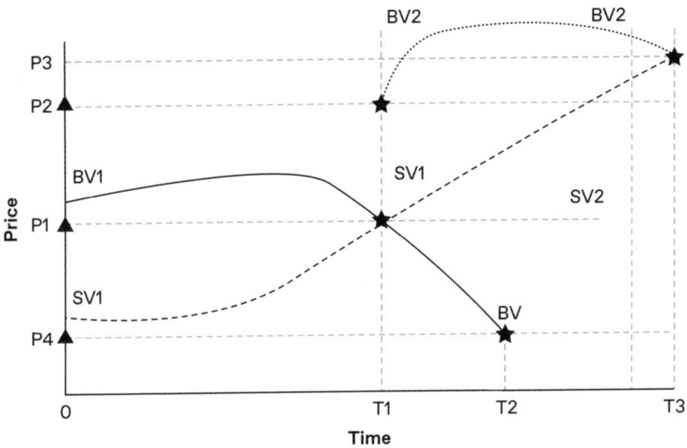

Figure 17
Development and obsolescence – refurbishment/redevelopment

This represents the decline in building value over the period T1 (20 years plus) at which stage the maintenance and management costs of the building have increased steadily. At this point, the site becomes more valuable than the building, and redevelopment occurs. Building value now moves to a new level BV2, with the life span of the building extended by a further period of 20 years plus to T3, at which time redevelopment again occurs.

Should development/redevelopment not occur, the building's real value will continue to decline until by T2 the buildings may now have a negative value. Here, while the site has a stable value (SV2), the buildings are in poor condition and demolition may be the most economic option. Typical of such situations is the operation of extended rent control attempted in various countries in the twentieth century. Rents, often frozen by legislation at historic levels, provided owners with neither an adequate return on investment nor adequate sums for basic maintenance of the properties. Decisions were consequently taken to make no investment in the property concerned and the most economic outturn for owners of such property was to allow dereliction to occur to such an extent that demolition became necessary.

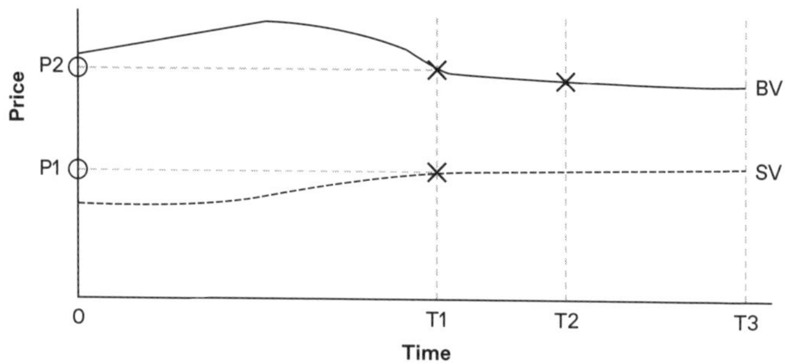

Figure 18
Development cycle stagnation

Stagnation within the development process also occurred through persistent weak tenant demand and prices, as demonstrated in Figure 18. In these circumstances, weak demand over time has ensured that by T1 the relationship between site value and building value has stabilised at a lower level, making redevelopment or refurbishment unprofitable. Low levels of demand for sites at this location ensure a lack of further investment, while a stable and low level of income from the property maintains its value at above this level, but without enough return to justify even essential repair and maintenance. Low returns keep the building in use but not well maintained, major refurbishment decisions are deferred, and thus a more gradual process of decay occurs. A typical life cycle of a major urban building is represented in Table 6, with one option being completing its life cycle refurbishment or redevelopment, and the alternative outcome being dereliction.

Economic cycles and property markets – future prospects

By 2019, in both the EU and the UK, a period of historically low European Central Bank, UK and international interest rates has led to a major inflow of capital seeking higher returns into property markets; central banks have expressed a fear that, without appropriate regulation, this could lead to excessive risk-taking.

Low interest rates pose the risk of both reviving and recreating the property bubbles seen in many EU states in recent years. Low interest rates on savings and government bonds are pushing both small and larger scale investors to seek property assets as investments, with prospects of higher returns and capital growth which appropriate property investments can provide.

Within the EU, the risk of property bubbles is potentially reduced by the ECB's Single Supervisory Mechanism regulation and monitoring of the capital assets and lending practices of the 129 most important European banks. In addition, given the recent experiences of the Great Financial Crisis, a degree of caution can be expected by governments and agencies with public responsibilities in terms of national macro-prudential authorities in each EU state and in the UK. This will probably involve a continued need for tight regulation of the banking sector and a cautious approach to loan ratios by house lending banks and agencies. This presents political difficulties, especially in sensitive areas such as retaining strict lending limits for first-time house buyers in markets where supply is restricted, such as London and Dublin.

Key indicators, property cycles and planning

The relationship of cyclical real estate markets and planning is both complex and often misunderstood. The idea of the perceived repeatability of economic and property cycles leads to expectations of chronological repetitions of economic and real estate patterns as indicators or explanations for public policy-makers today. Expansions followed by contractions, with varying time leads and lags involved, can overlook the changing dynamic contexts within which such change occurs and miss important significant shifts in context. For example, much of the analysis of the period before the GFC neglected to account for the fact that many of the key national and international pillar banking groups upon which economies relied were being led by incompetent and reckless management. In addition, public fiscal and monetary policies were designed to support and assist such market actors, rather than to effectively regulate them.

Key indicators of a property cycle include rates of employment/unemployment, inflation and availability of finance and interest rates. Statistically all these translate into key economic indicators of the property market and give a guide as to future trends. Other key indicators are all risks yields for commercial property and gross redemption yields on medium- and long-term government stock (gilts). With higher interest rates, development schemes become more expensive and developers' profit margins are squeezed. The tenant market will be affected as expansion becomes more expensive, although there will be differences between sectors.

During a market correction there is clearly little development control as the market processes withdraw and await the next upward cycle. Speculative development is an example of market capitalism producing profit opportunities in volatile markets. However, traditional views of market operations did not envisage the recent socialisation of losses and a state-subsidised reorganisation of the financial and property market to offer cleansed assets to new market entrants and funds prior to the re-entry of speculative capital.

This conflicts directly with previous ideas of the market's innovative and entrepreneurship capacities, including the concept of the creative destruction of capitalism from Schumpeter, where market capitalism is seen to provide a process of destruction through market actions which brings about the demise of whatever existed before and creates something new and more efficient. Such developments and processes in urban and regional development may not be more equitable, sustainable or in the public interest, leading to the need for a planning, regulatory and public policy input.

Recent strong market cycles have shown a fundamental problem in that the instability in construction and related labour markets is negative for both sustainable employment and critically for recovery capacities. The more comprehensive or integrated plan-led systems, while lacking the flexibility of market-led models, allow for a greater level of interventions at varying scales of regulation, intervention and direct investment. This is especially relevant in periods of low private sector activity when public sector investment and development can counter a downward cycle.

Such processes, however, require long-term policy commitments and policy frameworks. Their benefits can be seen in times when the priority is to stabilise or restructure markets. Switches towards such systems are therefore difficult to achieve and instead there is often a desire for a temporary or quick solution once a market correction has occurred. Unfortunately, as has happened in many regions during the recent market cycles, once a major correction occurs, the market or construction industry fragmentation can be severe, making a return to a well-functioning market in construction and finance difficult.

Property cycles and planning

It is also now clear that public policy and planning interventions in the recent past have been over reliant on short-term boosting of cyclical development activity. In the period since the 1980s, the UK and many jurisdictions embraced market-supportive reforms in terms of physical planning policies which prioritised property rights, reduced regulations and were intended to increase competition. Such policies have included outsourcing and privatisation which in turn have generated some successes in encouraging real estate development and physical regeneration. However, many political and policy interests are urging a rethink of such business models for planning and development, arguing that their focus on maximising short-term real estate and shareholder returns over their broader social impact is both unsustainable and contributing to growing inequalities.

However, there is no prospect of a return to any 'golden age of planning and public policy' – if it ever existed – and all international planning and real estate development models have their strengths and weaknesses. Internationally, it is clear that there will be a need for an enhanced role for planning and development management to ensure that a property market-led financial crisis will not occur again, and importantly, to improve the functioning of development markets for critical social and economic needs, including affordable housing.

The re-emergence of the state as final guarantor of the banking system, including the socialisation of the financial losses associated with property lending, marks a significant shift in public attitudes to both the financial system and state planning systems. This can be seen in relation to the issue of affordable housing, with a strong role of the state potentially re-emerging with demands for plan-led public sector responses instead of a continuation of market-driven or incentive-led approaches.

Chapter 6 Conclusions and Future Directions

Future directions and issues arising

Planning matters at the local, regional and global scale and many of the issues confronting current planners, policy-makers and real estate interests were summarised at the UN global summit on Housing and Sustainable Urban Development (2016) which examined policy and practice changes required following the adoption of the 2030 Agenda for Sustainable Development. In an explanatory piece[1] as to why planning for sustainable cities and regions matters, it concludes:

> ... To make cities inclusive, safe, resilient and sustainable ... What are some of the most pressing challenges that cities face today? Inequality is a big concern. 833 million people live in slums and this number keeps rising. The levels of urban energy consumption and pollution are also worrying. Cities occupy just 3 per cent of the Earth's land, but account for 60–80 per cent of energy consumption and 5 billion people are projected to live in cities by 2030 ...
>
> ... Many cities are also more vulnerable to climate change and natural disasters due to their high concentration of people and location so building urban resilience is crucial to avoid human, social and economic losses ... All these issues will eventually affect every citizen. Inequality can lead to unrest and insecurity, pollution deteriorates everyone's health and affects workers' productivity and therefore the economy, and natural disasters have the potential to disrupt everyone's lifestyles ...

> ... The cost of poorly planned urbanization can be seen in some of the huge slums, tangled traffic, greenhouse gas emissions and sprawling suburbs all over the world ... By choosing to act sustainably we choose to build cities where all citizens live a decent quality of life, and form a part of the city's productive dynamic, creating shared prosperity and social stability without harming the environment. The cost is minimal in comparison with the benefits. For example, there is a cost to creating a functional public transport network, but the benefits are huge in terms of economic activity, quality of life, the environment, and the overall success of a networked city ... Develop a vision for your building, street, and neighbourhood, and act on that vision. Are there enough jobs? Are you close to healthcare? Can your children walk to school safely? Can you walk with your family at night? How far is the nearest public transport? What's the air quality like? What are your shared public spaces like? The better the conditions you create in your community, the greater the effect on quality of life.[2]

Based on such aspirations and ideals, planning can still – as a discipline – contribute to urban justice and environmental quality, and evolve new tools of urban governance while functioning as a mediator between industry, development interests, policy-makers and community stakeholders. At a minimum, planning decisions should be taken based on an evidence-based core strategy, supported by factual evidence and market analysis. This is in the interests of the long-term sustainability of the construction and property sectors as evidence of previous development-led surges and corrections have resulted in unstable property markets, with shortages in many regions allied with high levels of vacancy in other locations and a dispersed inefficient development pattern. The absence of a commitment to and enforcement of enacted planning policies, along with the role of the political process in facilitating development, remains a severe challenge in planning systems with a narrow focus on development control. The alternative of pursuing broader urban management goals while prioritising the delivery of key societal needs such as affordable housing is a challenging, but worthwhile, goal.

Improving planning and property market outcomes

Attempts to streamline planning systems can be effective in encouraging short-term development activity. Examples of the directing of key infrastructure projects through centralised fast-track planning decision-making processes are now being augmented by the creation of strategic development zones or related initiatives which specifically focus on fast-tracking large housing projects internationally. This recognises that market-dependent planning systems have extensive power over development processes but often lack the ability or power to implement necessary development. This results in debates as to whether planning systems should move towards participation in actual development creation and implementation, rather than a continuation of a role of facilitating development. This argument is especially seen in debates over the shortages of affordable housing in many jurisdictions. Absence of action on affordable housing becomes a serious issue as to whether planning as a facilitator serves sectoral interests, elites and oligarchies of development interests or the broader public good and equity.

The earlier theories that planning should be a neutral process of public intervention to secure efficient and equitable patterns of development and a good environment have come under severe pressure in recent decades. Many planning systems have adapted to become more market-conscious and focused on economic development issues. The original focus of planning was on issues such as urban regeneration, urban containment and the protection of the countryside, housing in new towns and the rebalancing and distribution of industrial production. However, public policy objectives are now often not clearly defined but rather shifting and expanding. Many planning jurisdictions have continuously added to the original physical development objectives to add many new policy objectives, ranging widely from social and economic restructuring, environmental and sustainability issues and regeneration to business and economic development, community development and new local enterprise initiatives.

From an economic efficiency basis, critics question the costs and benefits of planning systems. Major periodic reforms have often been linked to the ideology of government, with changes in the composition and scope of systems based on ideological shifts rather than the effectiveness or otherwise of policies and initiatives. Such ideological policy shifts have involved moving planning policy towards favouring self-reliance and individual choice as reflected in market actions; efforts in the 1990s in many jurisdictions aimed to roll back the frontiers of the state. Since the financial crisis in 2007, the emphasis of planning and public policy internationally has moved towards servicing and stimulating investment and market activity. Conversely, in 2019, with economic stabilisation and recovery across many western economies, ongoing market supply problems have led to demands for a return to forms of public intervention, including addressing societal needs and challenges relating to planning and direct provision of public assets and affordable housing.

Sustainability

Many local and regional planning authorities have widened the scope of policy ambitions to include sustainability and clear environmental protection objectives which are reliant on both central government funding and market preferences. There are opportunities to learn from the evidence of local planning and development experiences and international trends. Alongside revised financing and financial considerations, the sustainable development agenda has become a major component within considerations of economic theory and practice. Policies and mechanisms, both mandated and via market-based instruments, are increasingly being used to both nudge demand and supply interactions and, in some cases, dictate behaviours. As a result, the fields of research endeavour related to environmental concerns (and essentially market failures) and to behavioural economics are beginning to cross-fertilise with the fields of planning and property economics.

Sustainable development principles have an increasing role in shaping demand for property, with energy savings, high standards of insulation and the need for regeneration of central residential locations increasingly recognised. Reflecting such trends, real estate markets are aligned in the promotion of sustainable locations with the gentrification of convenient brownfield inner urban areas and the promotion of passive transport modes. However, how the market reflects the capturing and valuing of the environmental benefits of energy and environmentally sustainable benefits in property assets is less clear. The transparency of outcomes in buildings grant and incentive schemes is often limited, and improvements can be absorbed into higher land and building prices over the longer term. For example, while the environmental benefits of home energy conversion grants are clear, it is also apparent that such grants can disproportionally benefit higher income households who may have had a capacity to carry out such improvements anyway.

From 2008 to 2019, the thrust of central government initiatives in many jurisdictions was towards austerity and to reduce funding for local authorities as part of efforts to reduce public financial obligations. This period saw a broader promotion of national sector-specific policy approaches in areas such as housing over targeting specific local area problems on a regional/local basis. Present local government structures in many jurisdictions have evolved as increasingly dependent on central government for financial support. Many local authorities also became heavily dependent on developers to help generate local property taxes and to provide local 'benefits' through planning gain. The inevitable tendency in planning and policy-making in such approaches is that a weak planning system can become involved in a facilitative process to smooth the course of development of the built environment. This can lead to a dilution of broader aims of planning and development plans, with a more entrepreneurial role for planning. This conflicts with previous aims that planning should be a neutral process of public intervention to secure efficient and equitable patterns of urban and regional development.

In terms of real estate development, a development-led approach with planning control creates limitations on developments and conversely monopoly value on sites zoned for higher value developments. It is this large profit or latent value which attracts development and investment interests. The distribution of this development gain obviously involves political choices. The argument that the community should have or share this gain is based upon that gain being mainly dependent on public investment in infrastructure and basic services, and that the gain results from community growth and effort rather than private activity. Consequently, the greatest pressures on the planning system are frequently by landowners, developers and builders seeking to profit from such development gain, or by affected local residents opposing local impacts of development. Speculation occurs in property with development potential, where the opportunity arises to purchase or take options on property through identification of a development opportunity not already discounted by the market into the price of that property.

In recent decades, the reaction of affected residents to planning policy has, in turn, become increasingly negative. The failures of implementation measures can lead to a loss of public confidence in future planning and increase the tendency to oppose all development, with often politically and emotionally charged campaigns opposing specific local development proposals. The absence of generic solutions to planning problems, the increased role of place competition and a liberal economic agenda can lead to uncritical acceptance of contested economic and financial concepts, whether appropriate to spatial development issues or not. Settled policy preferences in contested policy areas – such as encouraging increased agglomeration and larger scale and higher density urban areas, induced clusters of functional specialisation and flagship developments – can result in a focus on new high-end development and key infrastructure projects, with connection to more basic needs such as ensuring the delivery of affordable housing relegated in importance (Haughton et al., 2016).[3] These issues are summarised in Figure 19.

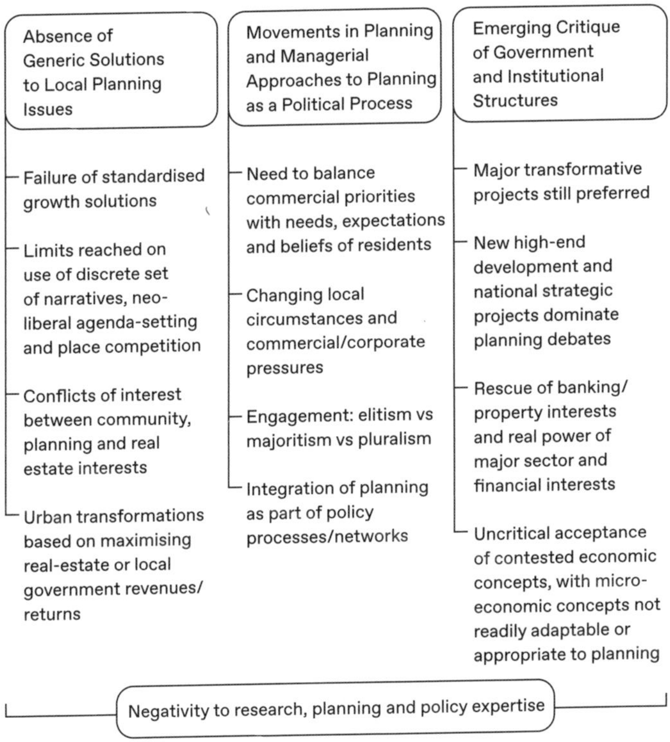

Figure 19
Issues for the future of planning and the relationships with real estate

Policy challenges in planning and the property market

Despite complaints regarding red tape and bureaucratic control, most private development interests favour some variation of development control as a planning approach, in that it can improve the functional interaction between various land users and prioritise favourable development conditions. Such support is also based on intervention being necessary for development to take place, in that the provision of physical infrastructure and utilities is necessary for new development. In addition, the regulation of future development militates against haphazard and uneconomic patterns of activity. Success is often cited in areas of strategic planning and infrastructure. Here, the state's organising capacity and resources are clearly needed with planning for improvements in transport utilities and vital energy infrastructure.

The dependency on capital and development interests for implementation significantly guides planning policy and gives dominant interests in the urban land markets a major role in planning urban areas. This dependency sees the state's active role reduced to dealing with both the infrastructure and public services needed to support development and ameliorating the socially undesirable consequences of economic growth, including residual demand for the housing of lower income groups unable to pay market purchase or rental prices. Such a role can involve major public costs, while sectoral interests potentially benefit from growth and development without sharing the resulting costs associated with new developments.

A challenge for urban policy and planning is whether the outcomes of such approaches are resulting in economic and social improvements. Next, if an aim of planning is to balance the benefits of development – whether across or within regions – in a sustainable and equitable manner, is this being achieved?

Clearly a range of policy interventions exist, from state ownership through to full privatisation of development rights in land markets. Simple solutions do not exist, and each policy approach needs to be evaluated on a principles-based approach, including the issues of equity, efficiency and democracy. Do adopted urban policy measures and planning initiatives contribute in a positive manner and make regions more equitable and economically efficient, while at the same time maintaining public democratic trust and acceptance?

We have looked at the relationship of real estate and planning. Examples of difficult issues arise in matching the public need for housing and basic services with housing market delivery. The absence of links with the wider public policy processes, bringing together real estate development and transportation policies, is also a clear weakness in many planning systems. Questioning of a total dependence on market-led delivery systems has been strong in recent periods as housing market prices are an increasing multiple of construction costs in many jurisdictions, as described in Chapter 4. It is clear that there is no single solution to a housing crisis experienced by many recovering regions at present. Each jurisdiction's housing crisis has multiple strands including homelessness, absence of affordable housing for purchase, a shortage of affordable rentals, and poor quality of older rental stock. The mix of problems differs on a regional basis and needs a suite or tree of policy approaches best adapted to the regional housing needs of each area.

National interventions such as those tried in the past – blunt tax breaks and grants – lack any focus and can be wasteful of funds, as much of the support simply flows back into higher land and property prices rather than addressing the intended problems. Attempts at policy interventions include support for first-time (FT) buyers, mortgage interest relief, and subsidies for purchase and rentals, all of which tend to inflate demand prices to higher levels without addressing severe supply issues. Public agencies can further inflate overheating markets by purchasing and renting from an already troubled market, just as investors and REITS can use their capital base and favourable tax treatment to purchase from the limited supply and then rent on at high prices to the local authority social housing sector.

Planning must demonstrate better outcomes to justify its role. This includes a need to restate the benefits of proper regulation, building codes, regulations, and health and safety; to reaffirm the environmental benefits of clean air and water, and less congestion. A focus on the implementation and delivery of key societal needs such as affordable housing and improving the public realm might prove more productive than a constant debate on widening the scope and responsibilities of planning without also addressing the resources and implementation capacities needed.

Broader equity and related issues

The distribution of income has become more unequal in most western nations and the urbanisation process globally has often led to decreases in poverty but increases in inequality. This inequality can often be traced back to the planning and land value capture processes involved in city and economic development processes from the period of modern industrialisation to today.

In many jurisdictions, a combination of most citizens as tax-subsidised homeowners with rising capital asset values in housing and a minority of excluded others developed and reinforced the spatial concentrations of deprivation which continue to exist today. The issue of inequality is strongly linked to high housing price issues in many cities, with resulting affordability problems. To what extent should land value capture be considered in urban policy-making? Are there more efficient ways in which urban authorities could treat properties' development values as distinct from their current use and occupation values? For example, planners in Europe could examine international examples of the distribution of development rights and the innovative use of floor area ratios in which land value capture is used for city/community purposes rather than individual wealth capture and extraction by land interests.

A clear alternative perspective on inequality is rooted in a critique of the structural economic basis of the role of capitalism in city and regional development by authors including Harvey.[4] Such arguments describe the established monopoly of neighbourhood as structured by economic class. This alternative view sees the most powerful economic classes controlling and internalising the advantages and amenities of specific areas while deliberately excluding problem populations and ensuring that activities producing negative externalities are hosted in areas with lower incomes and marginal populations which often depend on centralised social services. In European terms this is often debated in terms of both people-based income inequalities and place- or spatial-based concentrations of problems.

It is recognised that within the EU, the UK and internationally, the varying policy contexts and historical evolution of different city forms will require locally designed solutions and so a standard model or planning approach may not be useful. At a more advanced and integrated level, the Scandinavian models, rooted historically in social consensus, would view inequality as a broad societal issue linked to inequality in the general society. This approach leads to a wider debate on policies and tools, incorporating the need for planning as a central element. In these terms, the need for people-based and welfare interventions is often prioritised over area-based interventions, with a focus on real estate development. The evidence shows that area and property project-based approaches can lead to gentrification and displacement of problems. Such analysis leads to an exploration of the respective roles of city and national governments. Again, it leads to a knowledge that while many innovative policies are available at city and local area level, they need to be supplemented by general increases in the population's economic welfare to be sustainable.

The influence of the increasing internationalisation or globalisation of finance is rapidly changing the main economic drivers of development in many cities. Historically, in many European cities the importance of major regional companies and local banking groups with strong economic and employment linkages in the local area – Guinness–Dublin, Krupp's–Essen and Phillips–Eindhoven – was clear. Now, when economic, employment and financial interests are international, this can lead to a loss of regional identity and solidarity within city regions, reducing corporate regional engagement and social democratic values previously embedded in city development. A movement in modern corporate culture is that large corporations want to avoid paying taxes and have cities/regions compete for the jobs / incomes and employee taxes generated.

Policy and research in the planning and development fields have tended to focus on the concentrations of low income and deprivation, and to seek local solutions to problems which are associated with those populations. Alternative solutions could also be sought by the examination of concentrations of affluence and the actions and responsibilities of that 1 per cent, 5 per cent and 10 per cent of the population with significant power and resources. In conclusion the recent focus on the role of finance, bankers and speculative interests in planning and development processes is clearly justified. However, this debate could be broadened as affluent communities and suburbs also protect their privileges, often at the expense of less advantaged residents of the region. Finally, in discussing future trends in planning and development, we can also conclude that they can and will be shaped by unexpected transformative influences –such as the influence of Brexit – on national and regional development trends which, in 2019, remain unclear.

Notes

1 Public Policy, Planning and the Property Market

1. D. Harvey (2011) *The Enigma of Capital and the Crises of Capitalism*. London: Profile Books.

2. D. Kynaston (2007) *A World to Build*. London: Bloomsbury, pp 19–59.

3. UN (2015) Sustainable Development Goals Knowledge Platform: Cities – United Nations Sustainable Development Action 2015, available at: https://www.un.org/sustainabledevelopment/cities/.

4. The United Nations Conference on Housing and Sustainable Urban Development: Habitat III (17–20 October 2016). The New Urban Agenda, available at: habitat3.org/the-new-urban-agenda/.

5. DW (2016) Quito Habitat Conference Sets Goals for Urban Development, available at: https://www.dw.com/en/quito-habitat-conference-sets-goals-for.../a-36108962.

6. See https://sustainabledevelopment.un.org/post2015/transformingourworld.

7. OECD (2017) *The Governance of Land Use in OECD Countries: Policy Analysis and Recommendations*. Paris: OECD Publishing, pp 1–117.

2 The Scope of Alternative Physical Planning Systems and their Relationships with Real Estate Markets Internationally

1. I. Tosics, H. Szemző, D. Illés, et al. (2010) EU Plurel Report 2.2.1. National Spatial Planning Policies and Governance Typology, available at: http://www.plurel.net/; B. Williams and Z. Nedović-Budić (2016) The Real Estate Bubble in Ireland: Policy Context and Responses. *Urban Research & Practice*, 9(2): 204–18. DOI: 10.1080/17535069.2016.1174401.

2. Directorate-General for Regional and Urban Policy (1997) The EU Compendium of Spatial Planning Systems and Policies, available at: https://publications.europa.eu/en/.

3. ESPON/COMPASS (2018) Comparative Analysis of Territorial Governance and Spatial Planning Systems in Europe. Luxembourg: ESPON/EGTC, pp 1–40.

4. S. Shahab, J. Clinch, and E. O'Neill (2018) Estimates of Transaction Costs in Transfer of Development Rights Programs. *Journal of the American Planning Association*, 84(1): 61–75.

5. N. Brandt (2014) Greening the Property Tax. *OECD Working Papers on Fiscal Federalism*, No. 17. Paris: OECD Publishing. DOI: 10.1787/5jz5pzw9mwzn-en.

6. J. Abraham (2017) Just Transitions for the Miners: Labor Environmentalism in the Ruhr and Appalachian Coalfields. *New Political Science*, 39(2): 218–40.

7. OECD (2017) *The Governance of Land Use in OECD Countries: Policy Analysis and Recommendations*. Paris: OECD Publishing, pp 1–80.

8. J. Brueckner and L. Saavedra (2001) Do Local Governments Engage in Strategic Property-Tax Competition? *National Tax Journal*, 54(2): 203–30.

9. J. Corkingdale (1999) Land Development in the United Kingdom: Private Property Rights and Public Policy Objectives. *Environment and Planning A: Economy and Space*, 31(11): 2053–70.

10. Brandt, Greening the Property Tax, pp 1–18.

11. K. Barker (2004) *Review of Housing Supply*. Norwich: HMSO, p.7.

12. J. Muellbauer (2005) Property Taxation and the Economy after the Barker Review. *The Economic Journal*, 115(502): c99–c117.

13. J. Kemeny (2005) 'The Really Big Trade Off' between Home Ownership and Welfare: Castles' Evaluation of the 1980 Thesis, and a Reformulation 25 Years On. *Housing, Theory and Society*, 22(2): 59–75; J. Kemeny (2006) Corporatism and Housing Regimes. *Housing, Theory and Society*, 23(1): 1–18.

3 Development-led Systems and the Pivotal Role of Real Estate Interests

1. RICS (2019) An Introduction to Development Appraisal, available at: https://www.rics.org/eu/training.../an-introduction-to-development-appraisal/.

2. Home and Communities Agency (HCA) (2019) The HCA Development Appraisal Tool (DAT), available at: https://assets.publishing.service.gov.uk/government/.../DAT_user_guide_v4.pdf.

3. Trafford City Council (2019) Development Appraisal: A Basic Guide – Development Appraisal and Creating the Built Environment, available at: www.trafford.gov.uk/planning/development-control/.../guide-to-viability-appraisals.pdf.

4 Property Development and Financing Development

1. P. Wyatt (2007) *Property Valuation in an Economic Context*. Chichester: Wiley Blackwell, pp 1–59.

2. N. Dubben and B. Williams (2009) *Partnerships in Urban Property Development*. Oxford: Wiley Blackwell, pp 35–52.

3. A. O'Sullivan (2019) *Urban Economics*. New York: McGraw Hill Education.

4. R. Barras (1994) Property and the Economic Cycle Revisited. *Journal of Property Research*, 11(3): 183–87.

5. A. Baum and N. Crosby (2007) *Property Investment Appraisal*. Oxford: Wiley Blackwell.

5 Planning and Cyclical Property Market Processes, the Role of Market Prices and Property Market Analysis

1. B. Williams and A. Reynolds Feighan (2015) *Urban and Regional Economics*. New York: McGraw Hill Education, pp 185–201.

2. B. Williams and Z. Nedović-Budić (2016) The Real Estate Bubble in Ireland: Policy Context and Responses. *Urban Research & Practice*, 9(2): 204–18.

3. Williams and Reynolds-Feighan, *Urban and Regional Economics*, pp.185–99.

6 Conclusions and Future Directions

1. UN Sustainable Development Goals: UN Habitat III Conference, available at: https://www.un.org/sustainabledevelopment/habitat3/.

2. Goal #11 (and Other Sustainable Development Goals), available at: http://www.un.org/sustainable development.

3. G. Haughton, I. Deas, S. Hincks and K. Ward (2016), Mythic Manchester: Devo Manc, the Northern Powerhouse and Rebalancing the English Economy. *Cambridge Journal of Regions, Economy and Society*, 9(2): 355–70.

4. D. Harvey (2011) *The Enigma of Capital and the Crises of Capitalism*. London: Profile Books.

References and Further Reading

Abraham, J. (2017) Just Transitions for the Miners: Labor Environmentalism in the Ruhr and Appalachian Coalfields. *New Political Science*, 39(2): 218–40.

Barker, K. (2004) *Review of Housing Supply*. Norwich: HMSO.

Barras, R. (1994) Property and the Economic Cycle Revisited. *Journal of Property Research*, 11(3): 183–87.

Baum, A. and Crosby, N. (2007) *Property Investment Appraisal.* Oxford: Wiley Blackwell.

Bertolini, L. (2011) Interface: Planning and the Recession. *Planning Theory and Practice*, 12(3): 429–51.

Brackman, S., Garretsen, H. and van Marrewijk, C. (2001) *An Introduction to Geographical Economics.* Cambridge: Cambridge University Press.

Brandt, N. (2014) Greening the Property Tax. *OECD Working Papers on Fiscal Federalism*, No. 17. Paris: OECD Publishing. DOI: 10.1787/5jz5pzw9mwzn-en.

Brueckner, J. and Saavedra, L. (2001) Do Local Governments Engage in Strategic Property-Tax Competition? *National Tax Journal*, 54(2): 203–30.

Burwell, D. (1995) *Creating and Encouraging Alternatives to Sprawl.* Cambridge, MA: Lincoln Institute of Land Policy.

Cadman, D. and Topping, R. (1995) *Property Development*. London: E & FN Spon.

Central Statistics Office (various dates) Central Statistics Office Data. Dublin, Ireland.

Cheshire, P. and Sheppard S. (2002) The Welfare Economics of Land Use Planning. *Journal of Urban Economics*, 52: 242–69.

Cheshire, P. and Sheppard, S. (2005) The Introduction of Price Signals into Land Use Planning Decision-Making: A Proposal. *Urban Studies*, 42(4): 647–63.

Corkingdale, J. (1999) Land Development in the United Kingdom: Private Property Rights and Public Policy Objectives. *Environment and Planning A: Economy and Space*, 31(11): 2053–70.

Darlow, C. (1990) *Valuation and Development Appraisal*. London: Estates Gazette.

Department of Environment, Community and Local Government (DECLG) (Various dates) *Housing Statistics in Ireland.*

Dubben, N. and Williams, B. (2009) *Partnerships in Urban Property Development.* Oxford: Wiley Blackwell.

ESPON/COMPASS (2018) Comparative Analysis of Territorial Governance and Spatial Planning Systems in Europe. Luxembourg: ESPON/ EGTC.

European Commission (1997) Directorate-General for Regional and Urban Policy (European Commission). *The EU Compendium of Spatial Planning Systems and Policies*. Publications Office of the European Union.

European Environment Agency (2006) *Urban Sprawl in Europe: The Ignored Challenge.* Copenhagen: European Environment Agency.

Evans, A. (2003) The Development of Urban

Economics in the Twentieth Century. *Regional Studies*, 37(5): 521–29.

Faludi, A. and Waterhout, B. (2002) *The Making of the European Spatial Development Perspective: No Masterplan!* London/New York: Routledge.

Glaeser, E. and Kahn, M. (2003) *Sprawl and Urban Growth*. Cambridge, MA: Harvard Institute of Economic Research.

Hall, P. (1998) *Cities in Civilisation*. London: Weidenfeld and Nicholson.

Harvey, D. (2011) *The Enigma of Capital and the Crises of Capitalism*. London: Profile Books.

Haughton, G., Deas, I., Hincks, S. and Ward, K. (2016) Mythic Manchester: Devo Manc, the Northern Powerhouse and Rebalancing the English Economy. *Cambridge Journal of Regions, Economy and Society*, 9(2): 355–70.

Home and Communities Agency (HCA) (2019) The HCA Development Appraisal Tool (DAT), available at: https://assets.publishing.service.gov.uk/government/.../DAT_user_guide_v4.pdf.

Honohan, P. (2010) The Irish Banking Crisis. Regulatory and Financial Stability Policy. 2003–2008. A Report to the Minister for Finance by the Governor of the Central Bank, available at: www.bankinginquiry.gov.ie.

Jacobs, J. (1961) *The Death and Life of Great American Cities*. New York: Random House.

Kemeny, J. (2005) 'The Really Big Trade Off' between Home Ownership and Welfare: Castles' Evaluation of the 1980 Thesis, and a Reformulation 25 Years On. *Housing, Theory and Society*, 22(2): 59–75.

Kemeny, J. (2006) Corporatism and Housing Regimes. *Housing, Theory and Society*, 23(1): 1–18.

Knaap, G., Nedović-Budić, Z. and Carbonell, A. (eds) (2015) *Planning for States and Nation-States in the U.S. and Europe*. Cambridge, MA: Lincoln Institute of Land Policy.

Krugman, P. (1991) *Geography and Trade*. Cambridge, MA: MIT Press.

Kynaston, D. (2007) *A World to Build*. London: Bloomsbury.

Lohr, D. (2010) The Driving Forces of Land Conversion: Towards a Financial Framework for Better Land Use Policy. *Land Tenure Journal*, 1(1): 61–89.

McGill, G. (2010) The Effects of Taxation on Sustainable Development. *Journal of Local Economy*, 25(3): 251–63.

MacLaran, A. (ed.) (2003) *Making Space: Property Development and Urban Planning*. London: Edward Arnold.

Mirrlees, J., Adam, S., Besley, T., Blundell, R., Bond, S., Chote, R., Gammie, M., Johnson, P., Myles, G. and Poterba, J. (2011) The Mirrlees Review: Conclusions and Recommendations for Reform. *Fiscal Studies*, 32(3): 331–59.

Muellbauer, J. (2005) Property Taxation and the Economy after the Barker Review. *The Economic Journal*, 115(502): c99–c117.

Newman, P. and Thornley, A. (1996) *Urban Planning in Europe: International Competition, National Systems and Planning Projects*. London: Routledge.

Nyberg, P. (2011) Commission of Investigation into the Banking Sector in Ireland, available at: www.bankinginquiry.gov.ie.

OECD (2017) *The Governance of Land Use in OECD Countries: Policy Analysis and Recommendations*. Paris: OECD Publishing.

O'Sullivan, A. (2019) *Urban Economics*. New York: McGraw Hill Education.

Porter, M. (1990) *The Competitive Advantage of Nations*. London: Macmillan.

Ratcliffe, J. and Williams, B. (eds) (2000) *Development Properties in Valuations: Principles into Practice*. London: Estates Gazette.

Ratcliffe J., Stubbs, M. and Keeping M. (2009) *Urban Planning and Real Estate Development*. London: Routledge.

Regling, K. and Watson, M. (2010) *A Preliminary Report on the Sources of Ireland's Banking Crisis*.

Dublin: Government Publications Office.

RICS Valuation – Global Standards (2017) Incorporating the IVSC International Valuation Standards Issued June 2017, effective from 1 July 2017.

RICS (2019) An Introduction to Development Appraisal, available at: https://www.rics.org/eu/training.../an-introduction-to-development-appraisal/.

Sassen, S. (2001) *The Global City*, 2nd Edition. Princeton, NJ: Princeton University Press.

Shahab, S., Clinch, J. and O'Neill, E. (2018) Estimates of Transaction Costs in Transfer of Development Rights Programs. *Journal of the American Planning Association*, 84(1): 61–75.

Tosics, I., Szemző, H., Illés, D., Gertheis, A., Lalenis, K. and Kalergis, D. (2010) EU Plurel Report 2.2.1. National Spatial Planning Policies and Governance Typology, available at: http://www.plurel.net/.

Trafford City Council (2019) Development Appraisal: A Basic Guide – Development Appraisal and Creating the Built Environment, available at: www.trafford.gov.uk/planning/development-control/.../guide-to-viability-appraisals.pdf.

UN (2015) Cities – United Nations Sustainable Development Action 2015, available at: https://www.un.org/sustainable development/cities/.

Williams, B. (2011) Interface: Planning and Development Policy and the Recession in Ireland. *Planning Theory and Practice*, 12(3): 429–51.

Williams, B. and Nedović-Budić, Z. (2016) The Real Estate Bubble in Ireland: Policy Context and Responses. *Urban Research & Practice*, 9(2): 204–18. DOI: 10.1080/17535069.2016.1174401.

Williams, B. and Reynolds Feighan, A. (2015) *Urban and Regional Economics*. New York: McGraw Hill Education.

Wyatt, P. (2007) *Property Valuation in an Economic Context*. Chichester: Wiley Blackwell.

Index

References to diagrams are in *italics*